T0095680

Creating An Atmosphere *for* The Promises of

Melba K Wiggins

WESTBOW®
PRESS
A DIVISION OF THOMAS NELSON
& ZONDERVAN

Copyright © 2014 Melba K Wiggins.

All rights reserved. No part of this book may be used or reproduced by any means,
graphic, electronic, or mechanical, including photocopying, recording, taping or by any
information storage retrieval system without the written permission of the publisher
except in the case of brief quotations embodied in critical articles and reviews.

Scripture taken from the King James Version of the Bible.

WestBow Press books may be ordered through booksellers or by contacting:

WestBow Press
A Division of Thomas Nelson & Zondervan
1663 Liberty Drive
Bloomington, IN 47403
www.westbowpress.com
1 (866) 928-1240

Because of the dynamic nature of the Internet, any web addresses or links contained in
this book may have changed since publication and may no longer be valid. The views
expressed in this work are solely those of the author and do not necessarily reflect the
views of the publisher, and the publisher hereby disclaims any responsibility for them.

Any people depicted in stock imagery provided by Thinkstock are models,
and such images are being used for illustrative purposes only.
Certain stock imagery © Thinkstock.

ISBN: 978-1-4908-6190-6 (sc)
ISBN: 978-1-4908-6191-3 (hc)
ISBN: 978-1-4908-6189-0 (e)

Library of Congress Control Number: 2014921437

Printed in the United States of America.

WestBow Press rev. date: 12/02/2014

Lyrics: The Promises of the Lord Is Here

Verse1: The Word of the Lord is here;
I feel it in the atmosphere.
The Promises of the Lord is here.

Verse 2: The Power of the Lord is here;
I feel it in the atmosphere.
The power of the Lord is here.

Verse 3: The Promise of the Lord is here;
I feel it in the atmosphere.
The promise of the Lord is here.

Verse 4: The favor of the Lord is here;
I feel it in the atmosphere.
The favor of the Lord is here.

ACKNOWLEDGMENTS

First of all, I would like to acknowledge my Lord and Savior, Jesus Christ, who is the head of my life. I also thank my family members along with my sisters and brothers in Christ Jesus.

A successful relationship with God counts for eternity; everything else is perishable. All of our resources, time, and talents come from God. We should strive to use them wisely to bring others into the kingdom of God.

To

Cecil Wiggins
Corey C. Chieves
Terrell T. Wiggins
Jasmine M. Wiggins
Jeremiah I. Wiggins

And we know that all things work together for the good to them that love God, to them who are called according to his purpose.
—Romans 8:28

CONTENTS

PREFACE

The purpose of this book is to explain people's atmospheres. You can waste a considerable amount of time in your life trying to make things happen that only God can do. This spiritual revelation was given to me when I had nothing left but the promises of God to bring me out.

At that time, I realized how blessed I was to be able to spend time with the Lord and in His Word. The encouragement of God's Word along with His important principles have been the motivating forces behind this book. "Thou wilt keep him in perfect peace, whose mind is stayed on thee: because he trusteth in thee. Trust ye in the Lord for ever: for in the Lord JEHOVAH is everlasting strength" (Isaiah 26:3–4).

INTRODUCTION

God controls the final outcome of all that we do. We are accountable to carry out His works with diligence and disciplined training and not laziness. *Creating an Atmosphere for the Promises of God* is a teaching book that will challenge you regarding your responsibilities as a Christian.

God's plan for His people is that they have wisdom. Only when we choose God's path in life will He grant us wisdom. When we have that wisdom, then we have the ability and responsibility to create an atmosphere of high moral standards in every relationship. You can begin to relate to others and not be influenced by the atmospheres that they are in.

This book also challenges you not to accept what the world puts in your path in this life. You must be able to exercise your spiritual authority for yourself and others in your life. Creating an atmosphere shows and teaches you how the Word of God will deliver you from dead people and things in your life.

I once was looked at as dead because of where I lived. My family was living in a dead neighborhood. Because we resided there, we were looked at as just being people who would never have or be anything in life. But by studying the Word of God, I learned that it's never too late for God's presence to make a difference in your life. He will meet you wherever you are.

You have true deliverance in your life when you have total and complete control over the thing that once controlled you. You have the power within you to bring forth the promises of God into your life regardless of the atmosphere around you. It is never too late to make a difference in your life as well as in the lives of others. You have to be a determined person and study, mediate, and learn. You must not let where you live or what you have make a difference regarding what you know that belongs to you.

You were ordained to fight the good fight of faith. You must start by creating an atmosphere for the promise of God, regardless of where you are in life today. It's never too late to begin again. Whether you believe it or not, you don't have to wait for a new year to begin a new change. We have to say about ourselves only what God has said about us and not what the enemy says. Show others in your atmosphere that God is still in complete control in your life. I learned that faith is going to respond to you regardless of where you are or what you have or what you been through. You could be in a dead neighborhood, a bad marriage, prison, a hospital, or financial debt; you could be jobless, homeless or disabled. He is an on-time God. A change starts with you and begins in the atmosphere that you create.

CHAPTER 1

My Identity in Christ

Sometimes in life, you can allow the smallest actions to demonstrate the biggest impact. You tend to spend a lot of time paying too much attention and focusing on the damages that sin has already done in your life. You may feel that you have no control over it. There are a lot of things as well as people that we have no control over. But there are also a lot of things as well as people that we can and will allow to control us. There are people who are controlled by fears, habits, atmospheres, circumstances, and even the things they eat and drink.

Sometimes, we try to make people do only what God can have them do. The truth of the matter is that no one has more control over your life than you do. We often allow our thoughts, imaginations, emotions, attitudes, and words, as well as our atmospheres, to control us. Those are small actions that we sometimes do not pay much attention to because we are too busy focusing on the damages that they have already done in our lives. You can magnify the problems or the promises. If you take the time to focus on God and the promises that He has for you in your life, you won't have time or room in your life for anything less than what He said He would do for you. You must adapt a Godly mind-set and not focus on what has already happened to you.

Your past cannot control your future unless you allow it to. Do not focus on what has happened to you. You must focus on what you have left. God can do a lot with a little. The smallest actions will have the biggest impact in your life. You will say what's on your mind. "A fool uttereth all his mind: but a wise man keepeth it in till afterwards" (Proverbs 29:11).

You will do what you feel like doing, and most of the time, you will find yourself only thinking about what you see, feel, and hear when it is not the Word of God. "For as, he thinketh in his heart, so is he: Eat and drink, saith he to thee, but his heart is not with thee" (Proverbs 23:7). You will never really know how much control and power you have until you learn who you really are in Jesus Christ.

Learning your identity is a vital part of life. Knowing who you are now plays a huge role in your destiny and eternity. The Devil will stop at nothing to keep you from knowing who you really are. Satan will aggressively fight against the renewal of your mind; your flesh is going to fight wisdom. But it is vital that you press on and continue to pray and study until you gain measurable victory in your life.

The more time you spend with God, the closer you become to Him. Also, the more experience you have with Him, the more you trust in Him. "If ye abide in me, and my words abide in you, ye shall ask what ye will, and it shall be done unto you. Herein is my father glorified, that ye bear much fruit, so shall ye be my disciples" (John 15:7).

It does not bother the Devil if you know the Word of God; he knows it too, his assignment is to convince us that it's not true. You only become a threat to him when you are committed to what you believe. He will use anybody or anything to bring about distractions that keep you from growing in Christ.

This book is dedicated to everyone who has allowed his or her atmosphere to control him or her. Just as there are a lot of things that we have no control over, there are also a lot of things that we have complete control over. Knowing who you are in Christ, along with His will for you in the kingdom of God, releases into your life the revelatory knowledge of your divine nature along with supernatural manifestations. The promises of God will be brought forth in your life and in the lives of those you love. If you fail to know who you are in Jesus Christ, then you will not know God's will for your life, and you won't receive what already belongs to you. You will fail to keep what you already have been blessed with (family).

The book of Proverbs teaches us that we are only one of the two that exist on this earth. You are either a wise person who is presently seeking wisdom from God or a fool who rejects His presence and Word. "A wise man will hear, and will increase learning: and a man of understanding shall attain unto wise counsels" (Proverbs 1:5).

A wise person looks forward to hearing and learning the teachings of the Word of God. "A prudent man concealeth knowledge: but the heart of fools proclaimeth foolishness" (Proverbs 12:23). A wise person will keep the knowledge of God's Word in his or her heart, but a fool's heart will only bring forth foolishness. "The way of a fool is right in his own eyes: but he that hearkeneth unto counsel is wise" (Proverbs 12:15). A fool is always right in his or her own eyes and despises wisdom and instructions.

You are walking in either the kingdom of light or the kingdom of darkness. "The fool hath said in his heart, there is no God. They are corrupt, they have done abominable works, here is none that doeth good" (Psalm 14:1). God wants His people to have wisdom; therefore, there will be two kinds of people who will portray two types of paths in life. "Enter ye in at the strait gate: for wide is the gate, and broad is the way, that leadeth to destruction, and many there be which go in heaven. Because strait is the gate, and narrow is the way, which leadeth unto life, and few there be that find it" (Matthew 7:13–14).

The wise person seeks to learn, know, and love God and also wishes to be a peacemaker. The fool is wicked and will be a stubborn, selfish person who hates God and receiving instruction. This person does not wish to be corrected and loves disturbance. When you choose God's path in life, He gives you wisdom to stay off the broad path and stay on the narrow path. Wisdom has been made available to you, so when you don't know what to do, the wisdom of God already knows what to do and how to do it. His Word will only lead you into having a right relationship with Him in which you will only make right decisions in life.

Creating an Atmosphere for the Promises of God contains revelatory knowledge on how to prevent yourself from being controlled by what goes on around you and what happens to you and the ones you love. We should not allow our atmospheres and the cares of others to create any images within us. This book also shows you how the atmosphere that you create is quickly picked up by others. You want to create a Godly atmosphere.

This book is about standing your ground and positioning yourself for what already belongs to you because of who you are in Jesus Christ. Sometimes, we can waste over half of our lives trying to change the people we love and situations we sometimes find ourselves in. We can't bring people out of darkness; only the Word of God can do that. If we can't save ourselves, then we can't change ourselves or others. A revelation must take place through your spirit for you to see that in the natural, it is impossible to have control over someone else. But it's not impossible to create an atmosphere for the promise of God for someone else. Another person will have a will for his or her own life, and your will may not be what he or she wants.

The Lord has given people the power to make their own decisions; your life today is a result of your thinking yesterday. He does not force Himself upon anyone. But it's not impossible to create an atmosphere for the promises of God for someone else, especially if he or she is an unbeliever. Some people are so deep in darkness that they can't control themselves. But you do have complete control over the type of atmosphere that you create for the ones you love and those who come in contact with you on a daily basis.

There is nothing we want more than to see our loved ones, and everyone we come in contact with, to know Jesus Christ as their Lord and Savior. But of course, that has to be a decision that is totally made by them and not by you. Your responsibility as a Christian should be to intercede and create an atmosphere for the promises of God for the lost. One way of leading them to the kingdom of God is learning how to create an atmosphere for the promises of God for others. You must seek His hand and face in everything that you do in order to receive what already belongs to you and others. This allows Him to use you only for the uplifting of His kingdom. This type of atmosphere that you create is not just important, but also vital to survival on earth.

When you arrive in heaven, the atmosphere there will already be created. There is nothing that you will need to do, want, or bring with you. But always remember that you will not be comfortable in a atmosphere that you did not involve yourself in if you did not know the position you were responsible for there. That is just one of the reasons why a lot of people fail to attend church. The atmosphere of church is unfamiliar and not normally felt in their spirits or everyday lives. This tends to make some people uncomfortable.

People should not attend church to feel that they are in the presence of the Lord only when they attend church. Church is known as a place where Christians come together to worship the Lord, fellowship with other Christians, and obtain spiritual food for their soul. The presence of the Lord should be felt when others are in your presence outside of the church. "Wherefore, my beloved, as ye have always obeyed not as in my presence only, but now much more in my absence, work out your own salvation with fear and trembling Once you have given your life over to Jesus Christ you are then sealed with the promise of the Holy Spirit" (Philippians 2:12).

Ephesians 1:13 says, "In whom ye trusted after that ye heard the word of truth, the gospel of your salvation: in whom also after ye believed, ye were sealed with that Holy Spirit of promise." The Lord now dwells within you everywhere you go. Every hour, every minute, and every second, He is within you. He is omnipresent, omniscient, and omnipotent—not just on Sundays.

First Corinthians 3:16 says, "Know ye not that ye are the temple of God, and that the Spirit of God dwelleth in you." This is why you're required to create the type of atmosphere where God's presence is seen, felt, and heard in your life. People who are in your atmosphere should know that there is something different about you. When someone can't tell the difference between you and an unbeliever that's a serious problem. Romans 12;2 And be not conformed to this world: but be ye transformed by the renewing of your mind, that ye may prove what is that good, and acceptable, and perfect will of God.

There is a way to change the seen to the unseen, and that starts with allowing Jesus Christ to become your Lord and Savior. This will initiate a change of atmosphere that you should create for yourself as well as others. Living your life as a Christian demands a change in lifestyle as well as in your atmosphere. Being a true Christian is about living for God and not being ashamed of it. "For I am not ashamed of the gospel of Christ: for it is the power of God unto salvation to everyone that believeth: to the Jews first, and also to the Greek" (Romans 1:15).

You are not going to stand up for anything that you are ashamed of. You are not going to remain faithful to anything or anybody that does not have any value in your life. You are not going to listen to anybody who you know doesn't care about you. God's Word does not bring shame to your life; it delivers you from shame. "And ye shall eat plenty, and be satisfied and praise the name of the Lord your God that hath dealt wondrously with you: and my people shall never be ashamed" (Joel 2:26).

You are not going to be ashamed of anything or anybody that you believe in; that's why knowing your identity is very important. It all starts with who you know and how much you know about God and what He has done for you, not just what you can quote and don't have a complete understanding of.

You may wonder why Christians fail to have the abundant life that Christ died for. One main reason is knowledge. "My people are destroyed for lack of knowledge, because thou hast rejected knowledge. I will also reject thee thou shall be no priest to me: seeing thou hast forgotten the law of thy God. I will also forget thy children" (Hosea 4:6). In order for you to know who you are, you have to know what the Word of God says about you. In order to have what the Word says belongs to you. Then you have to know what instructions were given by God to you, like to tithe.

Malachi 3:8–10 asks,

Will a man rob God? Yet ye have robbed me. But ye say, Wherein have we robbed thee? In tithes and offerings. Ye are cursed with a curse: for ye have robbed me, even this whole nation. Bring ye all the tithes into the storehouse, that there may be meat in mine house, and prove me now herewith, saith the Lord of hosts, if I will not open up the windows of heaven, and pour you out a blessing, that there shall not be room enough to receive it.

Once you come into the knowledge of who you are and what belongs to you, the Word of God and obedience can only move you forward into the Kingdom of God. But if you are the type of person who just wants blessing without investing your time, talents, and gifts in the kingdom of God, your motive is wrong. You should want not only blessing, but also to help others find their way.

Book Notes

1. Are you a fool or a wise person?

2. What are some characteristics of a wise person?

3. What are some characteristics of a fool?

4. Describe your identity in Christ Jesus.

5. How can learning your identity help you create an atmosphere for the promises of God for others?

CHAPTER 2

Create

The Greek definition of the word *create (kitzo)* is "to form, shape become always of God." This applies to God alone; only He can become what was not there before, especially what is useful. God can bring about what was not there. When you hear the word *create,* you should automatically think of a process. *Webster's New World Dictionary"* defines the word *create* as a verb, which is known to be an action word. *Create* means "to bring about" and not "to make happen." Bringing about something means to carry or lead. Creation leads to an action or a belief.

In this journey called life, you learn to maintain the atmosphere that has already been created for you. Keeping up this atmosphere is necessary. *Webster's New World Dictionary* defines the word *necessity* as "the condition of being necessary, a requirement something that cannot be done without." Creating an atmosphere of trust in our heavenly Father is a necessity as well as a requirement.

You need to build a spiritual atmosphere in which God is a priority in every area in your life. "Trust in the Lord with all thine heart: and lean not unto thine own understanding. In all thy ways acknowledge him, and he shall direct thy path" (Proverbs 3:5–6). Trust starts in the heart and mind and then continues to line your life up with the Word of God. The Word of God has the power to change someone's life forever. He can change anything and anybody at any time. The Word of God has the creative power to change the seen unto the unseen.

You must first accept the reality that you were created to be like Christ. You are a spirit that possesses a soul who lives in a body. That is what being a Christian is about. You must live your life like Christ lived His while on earth. The only way to glorify God is to live a lifestyle that you were originally created for. We must always remember that our lives glorify the Lord. Have faith, be obedient, prayer, and apply the Word of God into your life. He died for you; now you live for Him and allow Him to live through you.

Having a Godly atmosphere will allow God's promises to flow into your life and also the lives of your family members. Creating a Godly foundation in your life that is based on the Word of God will allow God to work for you, with you, and also through you. You have to give the Father something to work with. Creating a Godly atmosphere brings about changes in your life, in the lives of those you love, and in the lives of those who you work or attend school with, your neighbors, and also your enemies. Creating will set a Godly atmosphere for whoever comes in contact with you.

One day, my daughter had a dental appointment. The young lady who was checking in the patients was not having a very good day. Things didn't seem to go in the direction she expected them to. She actually left me and my daughter out in the lobby waiting for one hour. She told me she was very sorry for her mistake.

I was later called into the back to speak with the dentist, and I heard her speak into the atmosphere, "I don't know why things are just not going right for me today." She spoke what she was thinking about. "It seems like I can't do anything right today," she said.

I spoke a word of truth into the atmosphere I told her that she can do all things through Christ, who strengths her. Philippians 4:13 says, "I can do all things through Christ which strengtheneth me."

She looked at me and said, "That was the most encouraging word that I have received all day." Just because some things can start off bad doesn't mean they're going to end up bad.

How could that have been the most encouraging word that she had received? Up on the wall, there was a printout with words of wisdom that included a word from the Bible. The words were there; they were posted on the wall. But they were not felt, seen, or heard in the atmosphere. The faith was there, but there were no works. There was no effort to put into action what was up on the wall.

The fact of the matter is that you have no faith because faith produces works, and that is why you can't have one without the other. "But wilt thou know O vain man, that faith without works is dead" (James 20:20).

One of the most vital characteristics of a Christian is an effect on moods and emotions—the ability to change the atmosphere. You can have bumper stickers, Bibles, and Scriptures posted all around. When you don't position your atmosphere for the promises, then you will never see the enemy defeated. But if you are involved in creating a Godly atmosphere of faith with works and obedience as well as prayer, you will bring about the promises of God into your life.

You are not working for the promises of God; they already belong to you. Your responsibility is to live a lifestyle that brings them forth into your life. As I began to observe the nurse working from that point on, she did a much better job after I spoke that word into the atmosphere. That taught me that God does not work by what you need; He works by faith,

You don't need to be having a good day. All you need is faith to know it's going to get better. This nurse simply applied faith with the works. She began to think about what I said to her. Sometimes people just need to be reminded that God is still in control. Just the words out of your mouth can create different things in other people's lives. What you say probably affects more people than any other action that you take in life.

Just think about it—someone is in prison today because of what someone else said to or about him or her. The anger of what was said to that person took hold and caused him or her to react in a very violent way. Then you have someone who lives a very successful life due to the fact that someone encouraged nothing but the best of them.

Ephesians 4:29 says, "Let no corrupt communication proceed out of your mouth, but that which is good to the use of edifying that may minister grace unto the hearers." Your words have the power to bring about one of the two actions.

"Death and life are in the power of the tongue: and they that love it shall eat the fruit thereof" (Proverbs 18:21). Words are containers for power; they carry creative power or destructive power. You have to know that your words can build someone up like a pyramid or tear someone down like a demolished building. The words that you speak frame your life and shape your future as well as the lives of others.

Sometimes we find ourselves building others up just to turn around and tear them down. "Let the words of my mouth and the mediation of my heart, be acceptable in thy sight, O Lord my strength, and my redeemer" (Psalm 19:14). The tongue is one of the smallest parts of the body but can do the most damage to us and others.

There are times when I have to ask the Lord to keep His arm around my shoulder and His hand over my mouth. You are to speak the Word of God into your life and the lives of others until it becomes a living part of your life—but the words that you speak have to be to the Spirit. Words that are spoken to the Spirit have to be from the Word of God because the Word is spirit and life. "It is the spirit that quickeneth: the flesh profiteth nothing: the words I speak unto you, they are spirit and they are life" (John 6:63).

One day, my husband and I went out to the hospital to visit an old friend who we both grew up with. About two days earlier, he had a slight heart attack. We sat with him and prayed for him and for others in the atmosphere. As we were leaving, we were stopped by the nurse who was taking care of him. She stated that he was doing much better on that day than the day before.

I then replied that he would be all right because he was in good hands (meaning the hands of the Lord and a caring nurse). The nurse had a look on her face that I will never forget. She said, "Thank you. I needed to hear that." The look on her face showed that she was touched by those simple words that I spoke into the atmosphere.

God knows what we need and when we need it. Others need to hear that life's mishaps and tragedies cannot be a reason to assume life is over. "Pleasant words are as honeycomb, sweet to the soul, and health to the bones" (Proverbs 16:24). A changed heart produces a changed mind; a changed mind produces a changed life. A changed life produces a changed destiny.

Change is the process of altering, transforming, making or becoming different. In order to have a changed life, you must have a changed mind.

When you transform the way you think and speak, only the Word of God can transform the way you live.

There are two ways in which changes can take place in your life. You can make changes happen or you can be changed. The most important part is to experience God and His Word in changing. When you allow yourself to be transformed by the Word of God, you are basically saying, "I want something different created in me, and I can't do it all by myself. I want the Lord's way of life." When you live God's way, you will experience a supernatural way of living.

You can only be changed by one of the two methods. If you are changed naturally, then that is called self effort. The works of the flesh attempt to accomplish through your own ability things that are the works of the Lord. Works of the flesh are your thoughts, imagination, emotions, attitudes, and words. These will be called self effort.

If you become changed, that is supernatural, which means that you have allowed yourself to be changed only by the Word of God and your hands were not in it. Trusting God to do what only He can do always leads to victory. When you believe the Word, then you will desire to have more of God in your life and applying the Word to your life.

God works where there is faith and works; then a change in your life will take place that was not made by self effort but only by the renewing of your mind. To renew the mind simply means to exchange your thoughts and beliefs for God's. You must adjust the way you think and not adjust the Word of God to be reasoned with. "For which cause we faint not: but though our outward man perish, yet the inward man is renewed day by day" (2 Corinthians 4:16).

If you don't change the way you think, your thinking will create the same atmosphere. Then you will begin to see the Devil as he really is—a liar, deceiver, thief, and destroyer of families. "The thief cometh not, but for to steal and to kill and to destroy: I am come that they may have life, and that they might have it more abundantly" (John 10:10).

The thief comes to take people's property secretly without the owners' knowledge. But if the owners refer back to the owner's manual (the Bible), they will be given instructions on how to take back what belongs to them and live a lifestyle that is pleasing to the one who created them.

The things the Devil said you could never be capable of doing will be done. The things the Devil said would never happen to you will take place. You will see that you are not the person that the Devil deceived you into believing you were. He lies to us and wants to trap, discourage, and snare us. He goes to work daily to produce discouragement, confusion, indifference, and imbalance in our lives.

When you experience an inmate relationship with God through His Son, Jesus Christ, you will see and know that He is not a liar—not because He does not want to lie but because He cannot lie under any circumstances. "In hope of eternal life, which God that cannot lie, promises before the world began" (Titus 1:2).

Remember that creating an atmosphere is an ongoing process. The book of Genesis sets the foundation of the creation of the world. "In the beginning God created the heaven and the earth. And the earth was without form, and void: and darkness was upon of the deep. And the Spirit of God moved upon the face of the waters" (Genesis 1:1–2).

The foundation of this earth was being created; it was a work in process. "And God said, Let there be light and there was light" (Genesis 1:3). God started the process of creation. First He started with the atmosphere; then he continued with the climate. "God said, Let the water bring forth abundantly the moving creature that hath life, and fowl that may fly above the earth in the open firmament of heaven" (Genesis 1:20). In the Bible, the word *firmament* refers to the visible arch or an expanse of the sky. In other words, the firmament might simply refer to the atmosphere.

After God created the atmosphere and the climate, it was time for the creation of humankind.

And God said, Let us make man in our image, after our likeness: and let them have dominion over the fish of the sea, and over the fowl of the air, and over the cattle, and over all the earth, and over every creeping thing that creepeth upon the earth. So God created man in his own image, in the image of God created he him: male and female created he him. (Genesis 1:26–27)

Man was purposely created to live forever. The first two chapters of Genesis are known as the book of creation. What would make you think that the continuation of that atmosphere that was originally created for people would not be necessary today? Humans still exist today; that's why the atmosphere that humanity was created in from the beginning is required today. That atmosphere was part of human survival on the earth.

What Jesus did for us two thousand years ago has an effect on our lives and atmosphere today. "Create in me a clean heart, O God: and renew a right spirit within me" (Psalm 51:10). David asked God to create a clean heart in him and renew a right spirit—not just any type of spirit. That only teaches you that a clean heart and right spirit must be created; you can't make them.

If David had the power to create a clean heart and right spirit himself, why would he ask God to do it for him? Obliviously the old way of changing was not working for him. Become a changed person by allowing God's Word to transform you. David could not do it, but God's Word could.

We cannot change other people, but the Word of God can and does change people on a daily basis. God is creating a new heart, character, attitude, and mind in you through the power of the Holy Spirit. Creation is a process; it can be a process of something good or evil, right or wrong, depending on who or what you ask for. "And that ye put on the new man, which after God is created in righteousness and true holiness" (Ephesians 4:26).

Putting on the new person who is after God is a creation process. It is an ongoing process in your journey called life. Life was created by our heavenly Father—spoken into existence by Him for you. And the words that are written in the Bible are to be maintained by you and manifested by God. You are to carry them on and keep them in existence.

You have the obligation to live your life only by the Word of God, not by thinking about doing what's best but according to the wisdom of God. Sometimes you can find yourself thinking about things that do not line up with the Word of God. Living by the Word of God is maintained only by you. No one can establish a personal relationship with God or seek the kingdom of God for you.

"O God, thou art my God: early will I seek thee; my soul thirsteth for thee, my flesh longeth for thee, in a dry and thirsty land where no water is" (Psalm 63:1). "But seek ye first the kingdom of God, and his righteousness: and all these things shall be added unto you" (Matthew 6:33). *I* and *ye* refer to you. No one has the responsibility for seeking the kingdom of God for you. No one can praise the Lord or experience the Word of God for you.

You can see God working in other people's lives. The life that has been created for you has to be maintained by you; that was God's original plan. You can worship the Lord, study the Word of God, and praise the Lord with others. But others can't do it for you. You can't make it to heaven on other people's salvation. There is no such thing as a give-one-life-to-the-Lord-and-get-one-free salvation card. You have to experience the plan of salvation for yourself.

The plan of salvation is God's way of providing His people deliverance from sin and spiritual death. God will take His Word and create a new creature in you. If you are changing yourself, then you are renovating yourself, and along with renovating come repairs. God's Word will bring about newness in your spirit, not repairs. He does not repair or try to fix your old spirit. He creates a new spirit within you. "A new heart also I will give you and a new spirit will I put within you: and I will take away the stony heart out of your flesh, and I will give you a heart of flesh. And I will put my spirit within you, and cause you to walk in my status, and ye shall keep my judgments, and do them" (Ezekiel 36:26–27).

The old spirit has been taken away, and you have been given a new spirit. The Lord starts to create your new spirit that will eventually align your soul and body with the Word of God. The new spirit has to be modified; it can't be repaired but must become new. Your spirit must be created—brought into existence.

It is not just necessary to know about God; it's also necessary to experience a personal relationship with Him through His Son, Jesus Christ. I had to learn that knowing about God and experiencing Him were two totally different things. Head knowledge and wisdom are two totally different things; you can know what to do but not know how to do it. The Lord will give you wisdom on how to bring the plan about.

Sometimes head knowledge will only tell you how to make it happen. That's why the difference is important.

You can know about a lot of things that you just don't understanding. There are times when you can mistake one thing for something else that has an entirely different meaning.

The cost of being a disciple will be you living as a Christian and not others living it for you. Becoming a true disciple is going to require a lot of adjustments along with sacrifices in your life. "And whosoever doth not bear his cross, and come after me, cannot be my disciple" (Luke 14:27). Being a true disciple of Jesus Christ is continuing in the life that was created for you. In the book of John, Jesus taught "Then said Jesus to those Jews which believed on him If ye continue in my word, then are ye my disciples indeed: And ye shall know the truth, and the truth shall make you free" (John 8:31–32).

Walk worthy of God in what He has called you to do. Come into the promises of God that you have already inherited. Bringing about these promises into your life will require a change in your heart as well as your mind and not just your behavior. God's plan for salvation works from the inside out and not the outside in. There has to be a change in your atmosphere and climate on a daily basis, one day at a time. The process of creation nevertheless can be longer for some and shorter for others. There is no doubt that creation is a process. But that is when the climate comes into action into your life.

The climate is the condition over average time. You spend more of your time out of the church than you do in the church. You have more time and opportunities for unbelievers to be in the presence of the Lord in your atmosphere. As a Christian, you are set apart and consecrated to God for His purposes as you begin to entrust your life to Him more each day. The world will start to notice a change in the way you talk, handle different situations, and carry yourself.

Create an atmosphere for those who choose not to attend church; you may not be able to have all your loved ones or friends attend church with you. But when you create the atmosphere of God, church comes to them. When others are in your spiritually charged atmosphere, they can sometimes find themselves doing supernatural things without even realizing it. They can do things like speaking the Word because they have heard you say it or maybe sing songs of praise because you played them. Perhaps others will even pray because you chose to talk to Him and not about others. Others' brains take in information that they are exposed to.

Always remember that you can't live a lifestyle that contradicts the Word of God. "I therefore, the prisoner of the Lord, beseech you that ye walk worthy of the vocation wherewith ye are called" (Ephesians 4:1). I received a revelation that when you are in the process of creating a Godly atmosphere, you are no longer forcing the presence of God upon unbelievers. When they are in your presence, they are already spiritually in the presence of the Lord whether they want to be or not. As you develop the mind of Christ, you will develop the confidence and ability to create your life and the lives of those you love.

"For who hath known the mind of the Lord, that he may instruct him? But we have the mind of Christ" (1 Corinthians 2:16). If you live the lifestyle of a born-again Christian, this should make unbelievers thirsty for what you have. Unbelievers need to know that God is still in the miracle-working business and on the throne. They need to know that there is nothing our God won't do for His people. That may not be something they have received knowledge of yet because knowing the truth not only sets you free, but also frees others within your atmosphere. They might feel the presence of the Lord is only felt in church. But the Holy Spirit dwells within, and you are the church.

"What? Know ye not that your body is the temple of the Holy Ghost which is in you, which ye have of God and ye are not your own?" (1 Corinthians 6:19) The atmosphere that you create also depends on what type of relationship you have with the Lord. Do you only have a relationship with the Lord when you need Him, when it is convenient, or when you feel like it? Do you turn to God only when you have the time or you need Him for something?

Or do you have a relationship in which apart from God, you can do nothing? Can you do all things through Christ who strengthens you? Is He who is in you greater than he who is in the world? Are you more than a conquer? The type of relationship depends on you and what you are willing to do for Him. "I can do all things through Christ which strengtheneth me" (Philippians 4:13).

John 15:5 says, "I am the vine, ye are the branches: He that abideth in me, and I in him, the same bringeth forth much fruit: for without me ye can do nothing." First John 4:4 adds, "Ye are of God, little children, and have overcome them: because greater is he that is in you, than he that is in the world." Romans 8:37 states, "Nay in all these things we are more than conquerors through him that loved us." Which type of relationship with Jesus Christ are you in?

What type of relationship are you in the process of creating for your life and others' lives? Any type of relationship that you're currently involved in is going to require communication skills along with time. The relationship that you have with Jesus Christ requires communication with the Spirit and time in His Word in order to bring about manifestation in the natural. You can have what Jesus died for you to have.

No matter how badly you want things for others, you must realize that they have to also want those things for themselves. Unfortunately, that has nothing to do with you creating an atmosphere for the promises of God. Others are going to want what you have. But sometimes others will not be willing to live a life that brings them about.

You can be as close to God as you want to be. Spend time in God's Word so you can connect with the Holy Spirit. "Now the Lord is that Spirit: and where the Spirit of the Lord is, there is liberty But we all with open face beholding as in a glass the glory of the Lord, are changed into the same image from glory to glory, even as by the Spirit of the Lord" (2 Corinthians 3:17–18). The time spent with the Lord and in His Word only brings about the same image He has.

You are going to allow Jesus limited access in your life depending on the type of relationship that you have with Him, how much you trust Him, and how much time spend with Him. If you give Him all of you, then He will give you all of Him.

Always remember one thing: creation means to bring about. When something is brought into your life, it is not done by self effort. Doing things with your own effort makes them works of the flesh. When you do things in the flesh, God's Spirit is not a part of that plan; you are not letting God be who He is in your life. Therefore, He can't bring forth into your life the promises that already belong to you. If you are making things happen, you will start struggling. Then you will become frustrated because things are not happening in your life the way you planned them.

Keep yourself where God puts you. You will trust in the Lord and include the Holy Spirit to bring promises into your life. Therefore, you will boast about it after it comes to pass, and God will not be exalted in it at all because He was not included in your plans. His plans always include us.

A planned relationship was created between God and humanity at the very beginning of the world. You did nothing to bring about the creation of the world or humankind. You certainly did nothing to bring about your physical birth. Why would God need your help in anything that He has created and is going to do for you? God does not need your assistance in being who He is. All He needs is your simple response to what His Son, Jesus Christ, has already done for you on the cross and what has already been accomplished for you through the blood of Jesus.

What you are doing is reconciling (to restore a relationship after an estrangement) a relationship with God through His Son, Jesus Christ. This atmosphere was already set for you in the Garden of Eden with God and people. The agenda is about picking up where humanity was cut off in the relationship with God in the beginning. When humanity was cut off from God, it was the spirit of humanity that died. That is why the relationship that you have with the Lord is through the Spirit. "God is a Spirit: and they that worship him must worship him in spirit and in truth" (John 4:24).

What type of atmosphere are you committed to creating in your life? God is in complete control of everything, and He does not need your help with anything. The only thing that God requires of you is your simple response to what has already been done for you. How He does anything is how He does everything—by faith. He is only waiting for your response to His Word. "For therein is the righteousness of God revealed from faith to faith: as it is written, The just shall live by faith" (Romans 1:17).

There was a time in the old covenant when people had to work for the blessings of God by keeping the laws. The old covenant God had with His people required obedience to the Mosaic laws. If they kept the law that was their part of the covenant, God would bless them. But now you live under a new covenant, which is one of grace. "For sin shall not have dominion over you: for ye are not under the law but under grace" (Romans 6:14).

The new covenant was created by God with His Son. That included the New Testament Christians. Jeremiah 31:31–34 says,

Behold, the days comes saith the Lord, that I will make a new covenant with the house of Israel, and with the house of Judah: Not according to the covenant that I made with their fathers in the day that I took them by the hand, to bring out of them Egypt: which my covenant they brake, although I was a husband unto them, saith the Lord: But this shall be the covenant that I will make with the house of Israel: After those days, saith the Lord, I will put my laws in their inwards parts in write them on their hearts: and will be their God and they shall be my people: And they shall teach no more every man his neighbour, and every man his brother, saying Know the Lord: for they shall all know me, from the least of them unto the greatest of them, saith the Lord: for I will forgive their iniquity, and I will remember their sin no more.

Now that you are living under the grace of God, you are righteous—not because of your works or deeds but because God has made you righteous. James 1:20 says, "For the wrath of man worketh not the righteousness of God." You are not living your life by the law anymore. "Knowing that a man is not justified by the works of the law, but by: the faith of Jesus Christ, even we have believed in Jesus Christ that we might be justified by the faith of Christ, and not by the works of the law: for by the works of the law will not flesh be justified" (Galatians 2:16).

You are not righteous because of the works that you perform. Doing right does not make you right. You are the righteousness of God by faith through Jesus Christ. You no longer have to work to be righteous.

When you were born again, you received God's gracious free gift of righteousness. You were made right by the blood and sacrifice of Jesus Christ. "For he hath made him to be sin for us, who knew no sin: that we might be made the righteousness of God in him" (2 Corinthians 5:21). What is right standing with Him?

You are made right with God. There is nothing you have to do to be righteousness. God has to make you right before you can do right; that will make a change in your life. You will live your life by faith and the leading of the Holy Spirit. "But that no man is justified by the law in the sight of God, it is evident: for, The just shall live by faith" (Galatians 3:11). If we live in the Spirit, let us also walk in the Spirit.

Grace is allowing God to work in you, for you, and through you. God is the only one who has a part. One does not have to participate anymore; one just has a simple response to what Jesus has already done for him or her on the cross. That simple response would be just to believe. Now God works for you—that is called walking in the finished works of Jesus Christ.

Everything you would ever need in this journey called life has already been provided for you. "According as his divine power hath given unto us all things that pertain unto life and godliness, through the knowledge of Him that called us to glory. Whereby are given unto us exceeding great and precious promises: that by these you might be partakers of the divine nature, having escaped the corruption that is in the world through lust" (2 Peter 1:3–4).

All you have to do is simply position yourself for the promises of God. Receive them by making Him a priority in your life, which will combine obedience with applying His Word to your life.

Book Notes

1. What is the definition of creation?

2. Can you create an atmosphere?

3. How do the words that you speak create an atmosphere?

4. How does the atmosphere that you create affect other people's lives?

5. Does God need your help or response?

6. Why is creating a Godly atmosphere a vital requirement?

CHAPTER 3

Atmosphere

The Greek definition of the word *atmosphere* is "surrounding a celestial body. Especially the one retain by the celestial gravitational field." *Webster's New World Dictionary* defines the word as "a surrounding or prevailing mood, environment or influence."

Putting something into action will only work to your advantage if you know what to do and how to do it. Knowing about your atmosphere is a vital part of this journey we call life. Who or what we surround ourselves with is a vital choice. All atmospheres are contagious, whether they are good or evil. You have experienced both of them by now.

If a good person stays around a bad atmosphere long enough, it will only influence them to do bad things eventually. If a bad person stays around a good atmosphere long enough, it will only influence them to do good things. Any two people will have different experiences. They will be in different places and see different things but not respond to them in the same way. They will meet different people and be influenced by different values and information.

Remember that being a bad person who does good deeds does not change your salvation status. Holiness is being of one mind with the Word of God. You can't be holy by changing your conduct. You determine the type of atmosphere that you create for yourself as well as others. Your destiny is chosen only by you. It's a choice that is constantly made on a daily basis. Whose influence are you under today?

Your atmosphere is composed of what's going on around you and what type of environment you are being exposed to. Along with living comes daily choices. Life is full of choices and options, but there is only one right way to live. You have the free will to choose a lot of things in your life. God has given us the power of decisions or choices.

You have the choice of whom you will serve or not serve. "And if it seem evil unto you to serve the Lord, choose you this day whom you will serve: whether the gods which your fathers served that were on the other side of the flood, or the god of the Amorties, in whose land ye dwell: but as for me and my house we will serve the Lord" (Joshua 24:15).

Remember, the promises are for you, and the choice whether you want God to manifest them in your life is yours. *Will I have time to spend with the Lord today? How can I set spiritual goals for myself? Will I have time to attend church today? Do I choose to live a Christian lifestyle?* Making choices means that you have options. Our choices make a difference—not just in our lives, but also in the lives of others around us. Choosing to follow Jesus Christ benefits you as well as others who come into direct contact with you. The type of choices or decisions improves the relationship that you have with Him.

Choosing to reject Jesus brings harm to yourselves and others. There are also times in your life when you are in a terrible atmosphere that you did not choose and the options were not yours at all. All you see are bad things. You seem to be in the midst of people with bad attitudes. Sometimes all you hear are negative thoughts of other people, and what you hear will affect your vision. You may be surrounded by people who have low self-esteem and do not want better things for themselves—so why would they want better for you?

People who say goals in our life can't be done should not try to stop the ones who are doing it. Perhaps you only see negative things happening around and to you. If you are in that type of atmosphere long enough, it will eventually start to wear off on you. That is why you need spiritual strength. It starts in the atmosphere.

You will begin to think like what you see, hear, say, and feel. Then you will start to do the things that you see, hear, say, and feel. Things that you see, hear, say, and feel are stored in your memory bank. That's why you have to be careful what you look at, who you listen to, what you say, what you feel, and who you are around. If you are thinking wrong, then it brings about wrong believing that will always lead to wrong confessing.

Negativity can be contagious; you must pay close attention to your atmosphere if you don't want to catch it. When the choice is not yours, unfortunately, that is still a part of life. There are going to be times when you will not be able to choose certain atmospheres, situations, or conditions to be in. That's unfair, but you serve a God of justice.

It's not your choice to be born with a heart defect or have only one working kidney. It's not your choice to have diabetes. It's not your choice to be a slow learner or unable to walk anymore. It's not your choice to be male or female or have only twenty-four hour in a day. It's not your choice to be born into this world or become old one day. It's not your choice how or when you die. But it is your choice to accept Jesus Christ as your Lord and Savior. This will be the ultimate answer to all the conditions and situations you find yourself in.

Sometimes you can worry about details in your life that you have no control over. While neglecting specific areas, such as attitudes, relationships, responsibilities, atmosphere, and the words that you speak, those are actions that you do have control over. "Whosoever keepeth his mouth and his tongue keepeth his soul from trouble" (Proverbs 21:23).

You can often invest too much of your time and effort into things and people that you cannot control. You can also spend your time investing into things or people that will not benefit your life. You are wasting your time with dead things. You must began to tell yourself, "I will no longer waste the rest my life trying to get something from someone that I know he or she doesn't know how to give to me."

How many dead things that do not produce good things are in your life? The choice is yours to invalidate (revoke) the type of atmosphere that brings forth nothing in this life. Sometimes people have a tendency to feel that making the choice to invalidate relationships will only make things worse than they already are. If you choose to live a life of misery instead of a life of victory, you can't blame others for your decisions. They were made by you.

How many dead people do you hang around? Ask yourself how much time you invest into the kingdom of God. Making that choice will eventually bring about much better results for you and others in your atmosphere.

The choices you make in life don't only affect you. They affect others who come in direct contact with you. "I call heaven and earth to record this day against you, that I have set before you life and death, blessing and cursing: therefore choose life, that both thou and thy seed may live" (Deuteronomy 30:19).

The choices that you make on a daily basis not only make a difference in your life, but also in the lives of your seed, which is your family. Do you love the Word of God enough to invest in it? Remember, we live by sowing seeds. You have to learn how to sow into other people's lives.

Consequences come with the choices you make. When choices are made, seeds are planted, and in due season, those seeds are going to reap the manifestation of those choices. But you don't have the ability to choose the type of consequences you will suffer in making wrong choices. As long as the earth remains, there will be seed time and harvest time.

Making choices also allows you to create an atmosphere for the ones you love. You can choose to be around people who talk too much about others or bring unto you total chaos. You can choose to be around people who steal, do drugs, drink alcohol, sell drugs, or gamble. You can choose to be around people who just don't do you any good at all. The wrong friends can only cause you to have the wrong thoughts, which will eventually lead you to accumulating the wrong things.

The wrong confessions out of your mouth will eventually bring forth the wrong things you speak. If you speak defeat, you will have a life of defeat. Confessions should only be about what God has said about you. Why would you say anything different about yourself? What people say comes from the way they think and what's in their hearts.

You can choose to be around people who only talk about the Word of God and the uplifting of the kingdom of God and others. You need to speak God's Word. What you think doesn't bless anybody—it's what you say. This process develops the proper image on the inside of you.

When you're in the atmosphere of people who expose you to a better life, it will only challenge you to do better. You can choose to be around people who give away things rather than take them away.

You can choose to be around people who had addictions but are now delivered from them. You can choose to be around people who have only your best interest at heart. The right friends cause you to have the right thoughts, which will eventually lead you to doing the right things.

Creating a Godly atmosphere for others rejuvenates them in the Word of God. Having friends and camaraderie benefits your future. When you spend more time around those with the anointing upon their lives, it begins to transfer into your life. There are times when we want to connect to people who makes us feel good about ourselves but are not good for us. "Be not deceived: evil communication corrupt good manners" (1 Corinthians 15:33).

A person mentality is the set of his or her mind; if you set your mind in line with failure, you will always have a failure mentality. When you set your mind in line with success, you will have success in your life. Sometimes success starts when you don't give up—you give your all. How you set your mind will eventually determine what kind of mentality you have. You will be able to expose others to this in your atmospheres.

If the people and circumstances that influence our mental processing and atmospheres are Godly, we find it much easier to fix our minds on Jesus. If you were raised up in a dysfunctional, abusive atmosphere, you may struggle with evil, carnal thoughts, imagination, emotions, attitudes, and words. "For to be carnal minded is death: but to be spiritually minded is life and peace" (Romans 8:6).

Speaking the right words will only bring about the right things in your life. If you talk defeat, you will be defeated. It actually takes as much energy to be in fear as it does to be faith. The mouth speaks things that are in the heart. Righteous people have good things in their hearts. Whatever you think or say will either add to or will take away from your life. "The mouth of the righteous speaketh wisdom, and his tongue talketh of judgment" (Psalm 37:30).

If you do not have a choice of surroundings, you still have the choice and responsibility to create a Godly atmosphere. If someone must be in your atmosphere, he or she should be revitalizing and not relinquished. Choosing an atmosphere in your life that will bring forth God's promises is going to require self-discipline.

Self-discipline is just one of the fruits of the Spirit. But all of the fruits of the Spirit are necessary in the creation of an atmosphere for promises of God. "But the fruit of the Spirit is love, joy, peace, longsuffering, gentleness, goodness, faith Meekness, temperance; against there is no law" (Galatians 5:22–23).

You're now under the influence of the Holy Spirit. The fruits of the Spirit are to be developed into your life; they are developed when you are led by the Holy Spirit. Being under the influence of the Holy Spirit is vital in creating an atmosphere in your life that will allow God's promises to flow.

The Holy Spirit guides you into wisdom and spiritual growth. In order for manifestation to take place in the physical, you have to learn first how to live in the Spirit. To be able to live a life in the Spirit, you have to walk in the Spirit. "If we live in the Spirit let us also walk in the Spirit" (Galatians 5:25).

In order for you to walk in the Spirit, you have to be led only by the Spirit of God. The Holy Spirit is going to lead, guide, and teach you as well as show you things to come. It takes power to be able to sustain this life. You must open up your mind and spirit to hear the voice of the Holy Spirit. Knowledge is power, and wisdom will be spiritual revelation that opens the doors to manifestation.

What exactly is power? It is the ability to act effectively and the authority to act. The power of the Holy Spirit dwells within you. How can you obtain this power? First of all, believe that you have power. It can only be obtained by the renewing of the mind along with spiritual revelation. It takes consistency to be powerful. You are not a threat to the Devil if you only believe, say or create an atmosphere for the promises of God one time. You have to keep doing it in order for it to make a difference in your life as well as the lives of others.

Some people tend to think the more that they have, the more power they have over others who have less. Power is in you, not in material items. There are things in your life that can only be done by Jesus—not by your job, how much money you have, or who you know.

In order for you to be led by the Holy Spirit, you must first have a relationship with Jesus Christ and experience His Word in your life. You have to be careful not to base your Christianity on the knowledge of just the Scriptures. It has to be based on the relationship that you have with the Lord and the foundation of His Word in your life. Sometimes people can think they are spiritually mature because of their knowledge of Scriptures. But they have no experience, understanding, or revealed knowledge of the Scriptures.

People try to live the Christian life without God. We can't live life without Him. And if you don't spend time in the Word of God, you are not experiencing a powerful relationship with the Holy Spirit. The Holy Spirit is not going to lead you into doing anything that opposes God's Word.

In your spirit, you have already received Jesus Christ's divine nature. When you do find yourself in a situation that you have no control over—regardless of the circumstances—the key to coming out is how you respond to it. Your reaction to the problem determines how long you will stay in it. People are known not by how they act when they are in control but how they act when situations are beyond their control.

A great example of this is how Paul and Silas handled their situation. "And at midnight Paul and Silas, prayed, sang praises unto God: and the prisoners heard them. And suddenly there was great earthquake, so that the foundation of the prison were shaken: and immediately all the doors were opened and every one's band were loosed" (Acts 16:25–26). Why were the doors of the prison opened? God inhabits the praises of His people.

Psalm 2:3 says, "But thou art holy, O thou that inhabitest the praises of Israel." The atmosphere of prayer along praise caused the doors to be opened up for them as well as others who were in the atmosphere. Regardless of the atmosphere or circumstance that they found themselves in that they had no control over, they still had joy and peace. Creating that type of atmosphere not only had an effect on Paul and Silas, but also on others who were in that atmosphere with them.

The people who were in that jail probably did not believe in the same God Paul and Silas believed in. They probably did not pray or sing praises with them either. But it worked out for everybody who was in the atmosphere that was created by them.

People will not always believe the same thing that you do. Others will not always look at things the way you see them or agree with how you respond to it. You still have the responsibility to circulate the Godly atmosphere for your surroundings and respond to your circumstances with the Word of God. And that method—along with faith, applying the Word to your life, obedience, and prayer—brings about the manifestation of God's promises that already belong to you.

God is excited in the atmosphere of our obedience and faithfulness. Once other people start to notice that His plan worked for you and there is no denying who did it for you, it becomes a testimony of what kingdom you are a part of.

Jericho fell because of the praises that were given in the atmosphere that Joshua found himself in. Again, the atmosphere was not working in his favor until he received instructions on how to create the atmosphere that would eventually bring down the wall. Joshua 6:20 says, "So the people shouted when the priest blew with the trumpets: and it came to pass, when the people heard the sound of the trumpet, and the people shouted with a great shout, that the wall fell down flat, so that the people went up into the city every man straight before him, and they took the city."

The people had tried different ideas to bring down the wall. But only when they received specific instructions did it work out. Like blood circulates to every part of your body, the Word of God circulates into every area of your life. The atmosphere that Paul and Silas found themselves in was not their choice, but the atmosphere they created was their responsibility. The doors were opened up for everybody. Their choice was not to complain about their situation but to praise God for what He was going to do.

No circumstances will change in your life if you are willing to let it control you and your atmosphere. If you complain, you won't have anything to gain. Complaining is always started because of the spirit of fear. You may fear that nothing is going to work out for you. Second Timothy 1:7 says, "For God hath not given us the spirit of fear: but of power, and love and of a sound mind." Psalm 23:4 states, "Yea, though I walk through the valley of the shadow of death, I will fear not evil: for thou art with me; thy rod and thy staff they comfort me."

But if you praise God, you will be amazed at what He will do for you as well as others. You can cause doors to open in your life and others' lives for good or evil, depending on what type of atmosphere you create.

My husband and I went to the hospital to visit his friend's mother-in-law, who had a stroke and had been in a coma for about two months. When we walked into her room, we felt the presence of the Lord in her atmosphere. Gospel music played in her room, although she could not hear it. She had plenty of get well cards that spoke words from God that hung all over her room. And there was a handwritten message on the wall that stated, "God is awesome." That atmosphere was created for the promise of healing.

We prayed for her and others who were in the atmosphere and began to thank God for healing her and others—and she begun to move. She did not wake up or say anything, but we knew that her spirit recognized our prayers because we spoke to Him. You contact the spirit with the Word of God. Her room created an atmosphere not just for healing for herself, but also for everybody around her in the hospital. She once could praise Him, but in her condition, she could not at the present time. There was revealed knowledge of who could do it. But the atmosphere that was created for her picked up where she left off.

The atmosphere that was created for her only had one thing to say about her character and the people she chose to surround herself with. They believed in the same God. She is a daughter of God. Her life definitely glorified the Lord. And the atmosphere that was created for her will bring healing to others around her.

You are not always going to be responsible for what happens to you. But you are responsible for the atmosphere that you create toward it. Even in this woman's unfair condition, she could not be responsible for creating that atmosphere. Her loved ones and friends along with her sisters and brothers in Christ did it for her because they knew the type of atmosphere that she was known for creating when she could do it. It takes being different to make a difference in your atmosphere. That would have been the type of atmosphere and response to her situation she would have chosen if she could. A couple of weeks later, she woke up.

Your atmosphere can cause walls to fall down in your life and in the lives of others. When you receive revealed knowledge that the choices you make will not just benefit you, but also others, it should stir your soul to make the right choice. There are different atmospheres in different cities, states, and countries—everywhere you go. There is no doubt that you are not going to escape the different types of atmospheres in your life that are in this world today. Romans 12:1–3 says,

> I beseech you therefore, brethren, by the mercies of God, that ye present your bodies a living sacrifice, holy, acceptable unto God, which is your reasonable service. And be not conformed to this world: but be ye transformed by the renewing of your mind, that ye may prove what is that good and acceptable and perfect will of God. For I say through grace given unto me. to every man that is among you, not to think of himself more highly then he ought to think; but to think soberly, according as God hath dealt to.

The word of God teaches you how your mind is to be represented and how you are to be transformed only by the renewing of your mind. Therefore, when you transform the way you think and speak, you begin to transform the way you live. Bad habits are your enemy, and they can keep you from being and living the life Christ died for you to have.

Once salvation has taken place in your life, the only part of you that is born again is your spirit, which is known as the inner man. Your soul and body unfortunately did not change. The renewing of your mind causes your soul and body to line up with your spirit that is now created in Jesus Christ. Your spirit is to serve God, so you are led by the Holy Spirit.

You are not changed by your good works or deeds or even positive thinking. Sometimes positive thinking can convince you that you can do it all by yourself. That is not what the Word teaches; apart from God, we can do nothing. "I am the vine: ye are the branches. He that abideth in me, and I in him, the same bringeth forth much fruit: for without me ye can do nothing" (John 15:5).

The change starts in the heart first, and it is sustained by the renewing of your mind. Focus on the Word of God and what He has said about how to live your life. Another person's opinion about how you live your life does not and should not matter. You are not going to be able to please everybody. Your objective must be a God pleaser and not a man pleaser. It's not about what others say about you, anyway; it is about what God said about you. It's not about what others say that you can't do; it's about what God has enabled you to do.

Romans 12 teaches on Christian conduct. There is a way that a child of God is supposes to carry himself or herself in this life. The Word of God teaches you not to carry yourselves like the people of this world. There is someone, not something, that makes you different from everybody else. That someone is the Holy Spirit, who dwells on the inside of you.

The Word of God teaches you that once you have given your life over to your Lord and Savior, Jesus Christ, and have been baptized, you are sealed with the Holy Spirit of promise. Ephesians 1:13 teaches, "In whom ye also trusted, after that ye heard the word of truth, the gospel of your salvation: in whom also after that ye believed, ye were sealed with that holy spirit of promise."

After you are sealed with the promise of the Holy Spirit, there comes a different way of living your life. It's a lifestyle that is separated from the world's way of living. Your entire journey is led by the Holy Spirit. Living and walking in the Spirit is living your life by the Word of God.

Faith is a matter of the heart and not the natural senses. God's Word must be believed in order for you to have access to everything that already belongs to you. That's why the atmosphere that we live in or choose to surround ourselves with is a vital choice. You can choose to believe His Word or not. You can choose to obey His Word or not.

The Christian life is lived by faith and not by what you see, feel, or hear if it is not the Word of God. Living life as a Christian is about living your life solely by faith and the Word of God and not by your natural senses. It's about what He has said about the different situations, conditions, and issues that you sometimes find yourself involved in. A change of atmosphere is going to be required for living and walking in the Spirit and not the natural senses.

You will have a totally different way of living. You live your life by faith, which will be by the Word of God. Nothing in the kingdom of God operates without faith. You are saved through faith. "For by grace are ye saved through faith: and not of yourselves: it is the gift of God Not of work, lest any man should boast" (Ephesians 2:8–9). You are justified only by faith. "Therefore being justified by faith we have peace with God through our Lord Jesus Christ" (Romans 5:1).

You receive the Spirit by faith. "That the blessing of Abraham might come on the Gentiles through Jesus Christ: that we might receive the promise of the Spirit through faith You also live by faith" (Galatians 3:14). "But that no man is justified by the law in the sight of God, it is evident: for, The just shall live by faith" (Galatians 3:11). You are healed by faith. "And the prayer of the faith shall save the sick, and the Lord shall raise him up: and if he has committed sins, they shall be forgiven" (James 5:15).

You also walk by faith. "For we walk by faith and not by sight" (2 Corinthians 5:7). It is obviously that the only method that the kingdom of God operates by is faith and not by your works or deeds. You have to create an atmosphere of faith in your life. It takes more than just reading and listening to the Word of God. You need obedience with the new nature when you create an atmosphere of faith with the Word of God in your life. You are preparing yourself to obtain the precious promises of God.

Faith has only one objective, and that is bringing forth the promises of God. Be a part of the kingdom of God where the only method the Word of God operates by is faith. It is going to require you to apply different principles to everyday situations as well as every area of your life and also your atmosphere. Choosing your atmosphere is more than a simple choice; it's a vital choice that is made on a daily basis.

You have to ask yourself, *Do I create an atmosphere of thanksgiving and praise in my life? Do I create an atmosphere of faith in my life? Do I create an atmosphere of love in my life? Do I create an atmosphere in my life that allows God's Word to take total control? Do I create an atmosphere in which I can be led by the Holy Spirit?*

Creating an atmosphere that allows God's promises to flow into your life should not be an option when you enter into the kingdom of

God as part of the body of Christ. Knowledge will be revealed after you study, mediate, and renew your mind with the Word of God and experience what the Holy Spirit has given you. There will be a lot of different things in your life now that will not have options, and your circumstances are not going to remain the same.

Love is the greatest commandment of all. "Jesus said unto him, Thou shalt love the lord and thy God with all thy heart, and with all thy soul, and with all thy mind. This is the first and great commandment. And second is like unto it, Thou shalt love thy neighbor as thyself" (Matthew 22:37–39).

Love is not an option. "A new commandment I give unto you. That ye love one another: as I have loved you, that ye also love one another" (John 13:34). The Bible does not teach you to love only those who love you. Next you have forgiveness. "Forbearing one another, and forgiving one another, if any man have a quarrel against any: even as Christ forgave you, so also do ye" (Colossians 3:13). Forgiveness is not an option; if you want your heavenly Father to forgive you, then you have to forgive others. When Jesus forgives us, He remembers our sins no more.

God does not give you an option to forgive. He's telling you how it is done as well as telling you why it's best for you. He's not saying, "Deal or no deal" or telling you that this is something you can reason with. "But if you do not forgive, neither will your father which is in heaven forgive your trespasses" (Mark 11:26).

It's plain and simple: if we want our heavenly Father to forgive us, we have to forgive others. There are no excuses or exceptions; it does not matter how many times another has wronged you.

It's impossible to please God without faith. Faith is not an option. "But without faith it is impossible to please him: for he that cometh to God must believe that he is, and that he is a rewarder of them that diligently seek him" (Hebrews 11:6). Faith is how the kingdom of God operates. If you want the Word of God to be manifested in your life, you must have a renewed mind, faith, and obedience. Faith is one of the requirements for obtaining what has been promised to you.

Webster's New World Dictionary defines the word *option* as "the act or power of choosing: a choice." You can't choose to live your life the way you want to live it and expect to manifest the promises of God.

You can't have one foot in the kingdom and one foot in the world. God does not negotiate.

How do you create an atmosphere for the promises of God? It starts in the heart. "A man's Heart deviseth his way: but the Lord directeth his steps" (Proverbs 16:9). "The Heart of him that hath understanding seeketh knowledge: but the mouth of fools feedeth on foolishness" (Proverbs 15:14). "Wisdom resteth in the Heart of him that hath understanding: but that which in midst of fools is made known" (Proverbs 14:33).

Second, this atmosphere is maintained by your mind. "Let this Mind be in you, which was also in Christ" (Philippians 2:5). "And be renewed in the spirit of your Mind" (Ephesians 4:23). "Thou wilt keep him in perfect peace, whose Mind is stayed on thee: because he trusted in thee" (Isaiah 26:3).

Before you have a changed life, you must have a changed mind. These are requirements for everyday living. You can create a Godly atmosphere by thinking Godly and right thoughts about yourself and also by choosing to not become easily offended or angered by situations, issues, or conditions that you have no control over.

Third, you must have faith to be sustained in your life. "Therefore we are always confident, knowing that whilst we are at home in the body, we are absent from the Lord For we walk by Faith not by sight" (2 Corinthians 5:6–7). "I am crucified with Christ: never the less I live: yet not I, but Christ liveth in me: and the life which I now live in the flesh I live by Faith, of the Son of God, who loved me and gave himself for me" (Galatians 2:20). "Behold, his soul which is lifted up is not up right in him: but the just shall live by Faith" (Habakkuk 2:4).

These are requirements to follow in life. You can create a Godly atmosphere by thinking Godly and right thoughts about others and choosing to not become easily offended or angered by different situations. Keeping a kingdom mind-set prepares you for situations that are seen or unseen "Finally, brethren, whatsoever things are true, whatsoever things are honest, whatsoever things are just, whatsoever things are pure, whatsoever things are of good report: if there be any virtue, and if there be any praise, think on these things" (Philippians 4:8). Where the mind goes, the person will follow.

Fourth in importance are the words that we choose to speak into the atmosphere. If your mind is focused upon God's Word, His will for your life, and being a faithful and obedient servant, that can only bring about two things in your life. One is victory and the second is His promises. When your mind is renewed, then you are going to change what you say along with what you do.

You are going to do what you think about the most. The more you focus on what's wrong, the more you are going to produce wrong things. That's why it does not benefit you at all to complain. The more you focus on what's right, the more you are going to produce right things. If you spend your time thinking focusing on the promises of God, then you can only be convinced to believe and trust in the Lord to bring them about into your life. "If ye then be risen with Christ, seek those things which are above, where Christ sitteth on the right hand of God. Set your affection on things above, not on things on the earth" (Colossians 3:1–2).

You can try to change by trying to change yourself. That would be considered self-effort. You can change by praying and asking God to help you change your life. Change in your mind also comes by studying, mediation, renewing your mind, and spending time in the presence of the Lord. In order for you to change your life, you first have to change what's in your heart. Whatever is present in your heart is going to be brought out. Nothing in your life is going to change until you change what's in your heart.

Nothing is going to change in your life until you change the way you think. If you don't change the way you think, then it will not produce a change in your life for the better. You have to destroy the old way of thinking before the old way of thinking destroys you. In order to obtain a different result, you have to do something different. The type of change depends on solely what you are thinking about. What you constantly think about will create an atmosphere of what you think of. The more you tend to focus on what's wrong, the more you will end up producing wrong things.

Changing your thinking will change the course of your life. "For as he thinketh in his heart, so is he: Eat and drink, saith he to thee but his heart is not with thee" (Proverbs 23:7). Set your mind, and keep it set on the Word of God. With the Word, you have the ability to think like

God. Bringing about changes in your life that are based on the Word of God shows whose influence you are under. It only brings about one benefit—victory.

If your life is under the complete influence of the Holy Spirit, your surroundings are acclimated to change if you find yourself in a position in which your atmosphere does not change. The Word of God has changed you. You will no longer respond to circumstances and situations in the way that you used to. Your circumstances will have to change due to the atmosphere that you obtain.

I strongly believe that we can allow different atmospheres to control us. That can happen when you don't give any thought to what you are doing or saying. Doing things like that would be considered a habit. When you are in the presence of people who have no control over themselves, things happen to you like saying certain things that don't line up with the Word of God. Sometimes it is better for you to say nothing at all than to say something that does not line up with the Word of God.

Every day, when you wake up, you should ask yourself, *What type of atmosphere will I create today for myself as well as for my family, friends, coworkers, and neighbors? Whose influence am I going to be under today?* One of my daily confessions is, "Lord, help me create an atmosphere that will allow your presence to be stronger in my life and felt by others who come in contact with me today." Another daily confession is, "As for me and my house, we will serve the Lord" (Joshua 24:15). And if it seem evil unto you to serve the Lord, choose you this day whom you will serve: whether the gods which your fathers served that were on the other side of the flood, or the gods of the Amorites, in whose land ye dwell; but as for me and my house we will serve the Lord. Is the atmosphere that you are in currently unstable? If your current atmosphere is unstable, are you allowing it to control you? What exactly does that mean? An unstable surrounding, condition, or person in your life is one that you have absolutely no control over. Anything or anyone that does not have a foundation in the Word of God will be considered an unstable spirit in your life.

The bible teaches us that a double-minded man is unstable. James 1:8 says, "A doubled minded man unstable in all his ways." A double-minded person is confused in his or her thinking and living. God will not bring about the promises upon a double-minded person. That would also include people in your life. Psalm 1:1 says, "Blessed is the man that walketh not in the counsel of the ungodly, nor standeth in the way of sinners, nor sitteth in the way of sinners."

Proverbs 3:6–8 teaches, "Trust in the Lord with all thine heart: and lean not unto thine own understanding. Be not wise in thine own eyes: fear the Lord, and depart from evil. It shall be health to thy navel, and marrow to thy bones." Trust in the Lord only; He is your stability in life. "They that trust in the Lord shall be as mount Zion, which cannot be removed, but abideth forever" (Psalm 125:1).

Sometimes it is good for you to have nobody left but Jesus. You will never know Jesus was all you ever needed until He becomes the only one you have left. He was all you ever needed all the time. God can do what people can't. It's better to put your trust in the Lord than to put confidence in others. People can have a history of failing you; it's good to depend on God, who never fails.

Some things in this journey called life are not meant for you to understand because you will never understand everything. You will understand some things, and you will just have to believe others.

Another one of our responsibilities is to take care of the possible and leave the impossible to God. Faith kicks in when you do what you don't really understand. Faith has a history of doing the unexpected. You are not meant to understand everything that you do or that happens to you. That will allow people to change their life to better fit the needs of others instead of the needs of just themselves. What's most vital is that we know that God has it all under control; He is in complete control.

You must trust in the Word of God in your circumstances, situations, and conditions and even for unstable people in your life. Life's atmosphere is not isolated from being changed. Your atmosphere will change depending on your relationship with God. It starts in the heart, depending on the changes that are created by you with the Word of God.

What does atmosphere mean to you? And why is it important to you? It's very important to you because the atmosphere determines what course your life will take. The atmosphere that you are now in can change if the foundation of the Word of God is a priority in your life.

But you must forget the past and look forward to the future. Sometimes we are born into certain atmospheres and find ourselves in different situations where we have no control. But we have access to who is in control through faith, which is how it's all going to work out for the better.

Someone in your atmosphere should know that you belong to a kingdom where you live your life only by a supernatural power source that is not of this world. If someone purchases me a gift, it is something that has to do with the kingdom of God. If anyone requests prayer, he or she will call me with the prayer request. If someone seeks spiritual advice, my presence is requested. That is the type of atmosphere that I am committed to creating in my life.

Being in an atmosphere where you don't share the same spiritual force with everybody will indeed be challenging. But never forget that all it takes is only one believer with the foundation in the Word of God to change the seen into the unseen. That atmosphere means you're surrounding a place or moment. The atmosphere was created by our heavenly Father by the foundation of the Word of God and must be maintained by you.

Jesus only created one type of atmosphere for anyone who came in contact with Him. He did not change who He was depending who He was around. Of course, He found Himself in the presence of unbelievers, but His atmosphere had an impact on other people's lives.

Jesus always created a life-changing atmosphere. Whoever He did things for walked away from His presence with a life-changing event. These people walked away not being in the same situations or conditions that they were in before His presence. Your responsibility is to create that same type of atmosphere for yourself as well as others.

Book Notes

1. What is the definition of an atmosphere?

2. Can you choose to create your atmosphere?

3. How is being under the influence of the Holy Spirit vital in your atmosphere?

4. What are some of the requirements needed to create a godly atmosphere?

5. Why does it make a difference whether you renew your mind or think positive thoughts?

CHAPTER 4

Climate

What is your climate like? *"Webster's New World Dictionary" defines* the word *climate* as "a prevailing condition or set of attitudes in human affairs." Climate is the behavior of the atmosphere. The behavior would be considered as the conditions of the atmosphere. Another definition for *climate* is "a region's usual weather patterns." The climate at any point on earth is determined by things such as the general change of the atmosphere.

Climate is better known to be the pattern of variation in temperature, humidity, wind, and precipitation. Climate can also be known as the pattern of the conditions in your life. Climate can be contrasted to the weather, which is the present condition prevailing in an area. The difference between climate and weather is that climate is what you expect to have, and weather is what you get.

As a Christian, you expect the promises of God in your life, and you're responsible for creating an atmosphere for those promises. But like the weather, the conditions of your atmosphere are what you get. The climate at any point on earth is determined by the general change of the atmosphere. That truth also remains the same in your life.

The climate has a pattern, and so does the life of a person. The pattern of a Christian's life is living in the promises of the finished works of Jesus Christ. Like the climate, that is what you expect. Now the weather is something totally different; it is what you get. What you get totally depends on the atmosphere over a short period of time. The condition of the weather causes the climate to change. The change comes about when the conditions of the atmosphere change.

The climate shows how the atmosphere behaves over a long-term average. What is the climate like in your life? What is the weather like in your atmosphere? What are the conditions in your life today? How is the weather in your climate?

One beautiful, sunny day, my husband and I took the kids to the park to play ball. As we played, everything was going wonderfully. We were taking turns shooting the basketball. When it was my turn to shoot, I bounced the ball, aimed it for the basket, and all of a sudden, my right ankle twisted. I heard my bones break, and I fell to the ground. I could not get up on my own.

That was like the weather—it was something I got. I did not expect it to happen to me. But it became a condition of my climate. When I arrived back at home, I did everything that I knew how to do in the natural to cause the swelling to go down. Over the course of that night, my condition became much worse. I could not even walk on that foot. I was confined to the bed, and others waited on me. The pain kept me up all night long. I could not lay my foot down without it hurting. Everyone was asleep except for me.

I was just lying in bed, thinking about the things that I was not going to be able to do and how this condition limited me in my daily routines. I had to cast down those thoughts. "Casting down imaginations, and every high thing that exalteth itself against the knowledge of God, and bringing into captivity every thought to the obedience of Christ" (Corinthians 10:5). If Satan can control your thoughts as well as your actions, he has you under his influence as a slave.

I began to call on the name of Jesus and speak His words of healing into the atmosphere. I had already started thinking about the activities that I was not going to be able to do. It was obvious that I had set my mind to my condition and how I felt. I didn't say things that agreed with God's Word or what I believe. I had to learn that if I have a need, God has the supply.

The next morning, my foot felt a little better. I could hop on it. I begin to start my daily routines in the condition that I was in. I could not let my atmosphere determine the outcome of my climate. I could not let it have any more control over me. The more I did, the better my ankle became. By the end of that day, my ankle was still swollen, but I could walk on it. My kids kept asking me, "Mom, how is your foot feeling?" I told them that my foot was healed.

I had to create the atmosphere of healing along with the attitude of being healed. That was the type of climate I needed to have, and it needed to be witnessed by others around me as well. Healing was my over-average pattern; healing was what I expected, regardless of what it looked like or how it felt. What would have happened if I had allowed the conditions of my climate to control my attitude and behavior? A lot of activities would not have not been completed.

Healing starts in your mind. I had already put limits on what I would be able to do in the physical. But there are no limits to what you can do in the Spirit. Communication was needed in the supernatural realm in order to bring about manifestations into the physical realm. The Spirit is the source of power. When I created a supernatural atmosphere of healing, it simply manifested in my body in the natural. Others wondered how that happened. None of my own efforts made it happen. "For it is God which worketh in you both to will and to do of His good pleasure" (Philippians 2:13).

I simply responded to the atmosphere in reverse to how I felt in my climate. That was my obligation as a Christian. My climate lined up with the Word of God. You are not to live by how you feel but by what you believe. When you enter into God's finished works, you turn off your self-control. All I had to do was believe it was already done and behave accordingly. I just responded to what Jesus had already done for me. My spirit doesn't believe what my body does; it believes the Word of God.

My family member had an accident at work and came home with a swollen knee and painful shoulder. Of course we did everything in the natural to help the swelling and pain. But this person only wanted to complain about the condition. When you complain, you won't gain anything. Complaining does not help your condition, climate, or situation at all. This accident happened at least two weeks before my accident. My condition and climate were much better the very next day.

You have to do something different in order to receive something different. Whether you believe it or not, that person just decided to keep complaining. When you complain, you will remain. There were two types of conditions with two types of responses. Therefore, we had two types of results. You can't allow the conditions of your atmosphere to determine your climate. Remember that your atmosphere is short-term, and your climate is long-term.

My daughter was born with special needs. The doctors said one thing about her, but God's Word said another. The doctor's said that she would only live to be about twelve years old, and she is now fourteen years old. One of the things that I taught my daughter to do is create an atmosphere for the promises of God in her life. The world will continue to tell her what she can and can't do because of her disabilities. She has the mind-set to know that she was fearfully and wonderfully made. "I will praise thee: for I am fearfully and wonderfully made: marvellous are thy works: and that my soul knoweth right well" (Psalm 139:14).

The Lord will show her what He can do, what He will do, and what He has already done for her. The Word of God says that Jesus is the author and finisher of our faith. "Looking unto Jesus the author and finisher of our faith: who for the joy that was set before him endured the cross, despising the shame, and is set down at the right hand of the throne of God" (Hebrews 12:2).

I taught my daughter how to live her life by faith and the promises of God regardless of how unfair life is to her. There is no reason why she has to stay in the circumstances she was born in. She is quick to tell anyone who will listen that she can do all things through Christ, who strengthens her. "I can do all things through Christ which strentheneth me" (Philippians 4:13).

My daughter's right hand does not open up all the way, but she was born to write with her left hand. God already knew that about her. She has had three open-heart surgeries but has more love for Christ than a person who was born with a healthy heart. Despite her natural and physical disabilities, she knows that the only person in her life she has a need for is Jesus Christ. What she can't do does not disqualify her from the promises of God. If there is something that you physically can't do, that does not disqualify you either.

When you enter into the Word of God, you will begin to find out more things that are right with you than wrong with you. That's why the

Word says that there are more things that are right with her disabilities than wrong. When you have unexpected troubles, don't resent them; just pray for wisdom. God has already supplied all of what you need to face persecution, adversity, and strife.

In this journey called life, you are going to have some disadvantages. Some circumstances will be unfavorable. If you give God all you have—regardless of what that is—He will give you all of Him and all that already belongs to you. My daughter has been taught to create her atmosphere and maintain the climate within in her ability.

In short, climate is the description of the long-term pattern of weather in a particular area. But in the supernatural, the long-term pattern shows the climate in every area of your life. What is the climate like in your atmosphere? The type of weather that a country or region has can be hot, cold, mild, or warm. The Word of God's definition of a supernatural climate is a person's behavior in a situation. You are to act like you believe.

Plain and simple, your attitude toward a problem always agrees with how you respond to it. The weather changes on a daily basis. The weather can be hot, cold, windy, or rainy. The type of living conditions and circumstance in a person's life can also change. They can change like the weather—minute to minute, day to day, or even season to season.

The climate is the long-term behavior of your atmosphere, the pattern of your conditions, and circumstances in the atmosphere that you are in. When you talk about creating an atmosphere, that comes along with the climate also. You must behave in a way that lines up with what you create. If you are near someone who has a negative attitude, his or her behavior will line up with what he or she believes.

In life, you may expect one thing, but you can sometimes get something else. You expect the promises of God to be manifested in your life. That is the pattern of a Christian's atmosphere. Talking about climate change starts with creating a new and different atmosphere. The climate and atmosphere go together. You can't have one without the other, just like you can't have salvation without believing Jesus Christ died for your sins. Neither can you have faith without works.

There comes a time in your life when you need a climate change in your atmosphere. You may say, "Okay! What exactly is a climate change in my life?" A climate change is considered to be a long-term shift in every area in your life, which will be your behavior. God's will for you is to have success in every area of your life. Like the weather is a pattern in your everyday life, living in the promises of God is also the pattern of a Christian life.

The weather is limited to location—regions. The Word of God does not put any limits on any area of your life. Sometimes you put limits on yourself depending on the type relationship that you have with Him. The shift is measured by changes in your atmosphere as well as actions in your life that are in line with the Word of God. A climate change occurs only when your entire life is changed by the Word of God. You have to remind yourself daily that promotion comes from God and not people.

A weather condition also causes the climate to change. Your climate changes by releasing the Word of God into the atmosphere to work for you. But don't forget that you have to first create the atmosphere for the promises. The Word of God is released and applied to your everyday living. But climate change starts with the atmosphere. It starts with your surroundings and environment. Both natural and supernatural factors that can cause climate change in your life are called climate forcing since they push or force the climate to shift to a new status.

What causes the climate to change? The increased concentration of atmospheric particles blocks out any and everything that does not line up with the Word of God in your life. You behave according to what you believe. Plenty of people tell you to speak the Word of God into your atmosphere. You then begin to think that it is just that simple. But what they forget to tell you is that if your behavior and attitude toward what you speak do not line up with what you confess, they have no power. You are not a threat to the Devil if you do it only one time.

When you increase God's Word in your life, you have the capability and clarification to overcome evil and close the doors to obstacles that would hinder God's promises from flowing into your life. Open up doors for blessing that will chase you down.

What can you do about the climate change in your life? Take action on the Word of God, living your life according not to what you see, hear, or feel but only by the wisdom of the Word. The leading of the Holy

Spirit can make not only your life change for the better, but also that of everyone who comes in contact with you and the Godly atmosphere that you have created in your life.

Adaptation involves taking action to minimize the negative surrounding of your atmosphere. The change of your atmosphere will also bring about a climate change. You can't change what you don't confront. And before you try to change other people's lives, you first have to confront your own issues. Realize that we can't change ourselves or other people.

Confrontation always requires action to be taken. Putting the Word of God to work in your life takes action. It is a vital part of changing your life as well as your climate. It is not the only part but one of the parts that is required for change. What happens when the climate changes? When the climate begins to change, things begin to happen in your life that never would have happened if you did not apply the Word of God along with the correct behavior and attitude in your atmosphere.

First of all, your relationship with the Lord will change; you will become closer to Him. People as well as situations in your life begin to turn around for the better. Increasing the revealed knowledge of the Word of God and applying what you have learned to your life brings about healing, deliverance, financial freedom, joy, peace, and protection. There will be changes in bad habits, environmental surroundings, and social connections. There will also be changes in relationships and communication skills. All those changes will accrue because a change was created within you.

Climate change may occur over long-term timescales from a variety of factors in your life. Creating an atmosphere in your life that allows God's promises to flow has to be set by the Word of God. The atmosphere has to be set and also maintained by you with only the Word of God. You have to basically position yourself for the promises of God. Remember that positioning yourself and speaking the promises are two totally different things. First you have to create an atmosphere; then it will start to bring about changes in your climate. Do not bring these about by self-effort. Start creating the type of atmosphere, and the usual patterns of being a Christian will be brought about. You want to live a life that will glorify the Lord.

The weather has certain conditions that put limits on to your life and activities. Sometimes if you have plans for an activity and the weather is not what you expected, it is what you get. Perhaps your plans can be canceled, or maybe you will not allow the conditions to hinder what you had planned. It is the same with the Word of God, depending on the type of relationship you have with Him.

The meteorologist studies the weather and they can basically tell you what to expect for a day or even the week to come. If you are being led by the Spirit of God, there will be no limits to what God can or will do, depending on your relationship with Him. The advantage that you have over the meteorologist is that the Word of God tells you the outcome for your life if you are saved or unsaved. It gives you your forecast for eternity. You already know way ahead of time what conditions to expect. And when certain unexpected conditions happen, knowledge on how to respond to them is revealed. It also gives you a forecast on what your life is going to be like whether or not you believe or seek Him.

Climate is what you expect; however, it is the average of weather over time and space. An easy way to remember the difference between the atmosphere and climate would be that climate is what you expect, like a very hot summer. The climate is the behavior or conditions of the atmosphere. When the patterns of the Word of God are followed, you already know what to expect. The promises of God are what you expect because they already belong to you.

Atmosphere is what you get—like a rainy day. Your atmosphere is your surroundings, prevailing mood, environment, or influence. You can use the weather as an example of the condition of the atmosphere and how it changes from one day to another. It may be hot one day and cold another day. Or perhaps it will rain one day and be clear the next day. You could be happy one day and sad one day. You could be in a negative situation or even in the presence of negative people, or you could be in the presence of positive people.

Creating a Godly atmosphere in your life is a necessity. Climate brings about the over time average of God's promises in your life. The weather is like the conditions of our lives day to day. The climate is what you would expect your life to be while creating the Godly atmosphere.

What do you expect? You expect the promises of that abundant life that Jesus died for you to have. Who knows what the atmosphere or condition may bring; it's unpredictable, erratic, and ever-changing. And while we may never know exactly what the atmosphere or conditions have in store for us in the future, we now know how to create our atmospheres along with the climate.

The one thing we know about the climate is how to be ready for it. To have a behavior, we must act like we already have it and not complain or doubt whether something will take place or not. If the forecast is for a rainy day, you will prepare yourself with an umbrella or a raincoat. If the forecast is for a very cold day, you will prepare yourself with a coat, hat, and gloves.

The teachings and instructions of God's Word prepare you for the supernatural conditions of life as well. They make you clean without self-effort. The Word of God and faith together give you the confidence to face any kind of atmosphere or condition. Using the Word of God in your life can only take you forward and not backward. The light of day does not refuse to shine because of the atmosphere; it comes up anyway. It comes up if it rains or is cold. The light of day remains the same; you should in your climate as well.

The state of Florida is known for its sunny climate and beautiful beaches. With that information, the visitors as well as citizens of that state are always well prepared for that climate. The kingdom of God is known for its grace, mercy, and abundance (ample supply), and God's children are prepared for that climate also. It's time for you to start paying very close attention to your atmosphere as well the climate. Begin adapting to the changes in your atmosphere and climate every day.

Melba K Wiggins

Book Notes

1. What is the definition of climate?

2. What does climate mean to you?

3. How do climate and atmosphere connect in your life?

4. Can you have one without the other?

5. How does climate have an effect on your behavior and attitude?

CHAPTER 5

Promise

The Hebrew word for *promise* is "berit." The Hebrew worldview of *berit* is that it is between God and His chosen people. The word translates into English as "covenant." A covenant is an agreement between two parties. There are two types of covenants: conditional and unconditional. A conditional covenant is an agreement that binds both parties for its fulfillment. Both parties agree to fulfill certain conditions. An unconditional covenant is an agreement that is between two parties, but only one of the two has to do something.

There are five great Bible covenants. Before the time of Abraham, God made a covenant with Noah assuring Noah that God would never again destroy the world by flood. "And God said unto Noah, This is the token of the covenant, which I have established between me and all flesh that is upon the earth" (Genesis 9:17).

Noah lived in a time when the whole world was filled with violence and corruption. "And God saw that the wickedness of man was great in the earth and that every imagination of the thoughts of his heart was only evil continually" (Genesis 6:5). Noah did not allow the evil that was present in his atmosphere to rob him of fellowship with God. Noah continued to obtain the climate and behavior of his atmosphere that was in opposition to God.

The Abraham covenant is an unconditional covenant. God made promises to Abraham that required nothing of Abraham.

In the same day the Lord made a covenant with Abram, saying, Unto thy seed have me given this land, from the river of Egypt unto the great river, the river Euphrates. The Kenites and the Kenizites and the Kadmonites. And the Hittites and the Perizzites, and the Rephaims, And the Amorites, and the Canaanites and the Girgashites, and the Jebusites. (Genesis 15:18–21)

There are three main features in the Abraham covenant; one is the promise of land. "Now the Lord had said unto Abram, Get thee out of thy country, and from thy kindred, and from thy father house, unto a land that I will shew thee" (Genesis 12:1). There was also a promise of descents. "And I will make of thee a great nation, and I will bless thee, and make thy name great: and thou shalt be a blessing" (Genesis 12:2). Third was a promise of blessings and redemption. "And I will bless them that bless thee, and curse him that curseth thee: and in thee shall all families of the earth be blessed" (Genesis 12:3).

The Moses covenant is a conditional covenant made between God and the nation of Israel on Mount Sinai. "Now therefore, if ye will obey my voice indeed, and keep my covenant, then ye shall be a peculiar treasure unto me above all people: for all the earth is mine" (Exodus 19:5).

This covenant was between God and Israel. You and I are not parties in that covenant and never have been. The Ten Commandments are the foundation of the covenant but not the entirely of it. There are more than six hundred laws that were given to Moses. The Moses covenant did not take away sin.

> For the law having a shadow of good things to come, and not the very image of the things of, can never with those sacrifices which they offered year by year continually make the comers thereunto perfect. For then would they not have ceased to be offered? Because that the worshippers once purged should have had no more conscience of sins. But those sacrifices there is a remembrance again made of sins every year. For it is not possible that the blood of bulls and of goats should take away sins. (Hebrews 10:1–4)

Covenants were traditionally made with the blood of a sacrifice. The new covenant was also made with sacrificial blood. "Of hoe much sorer punishment, suppose ye, shall he be thought worthy, who hath counted the blood of the covenant, wherewith he was sanctified, an unholy thing, and hath done despite unto the Spirit of grace?" (Hebrews 10:29) It was only the blood of Jesus of the new covenant that sanctified us.

The laws were given to people to make them conscious of their sin. If there were not laws, how they would have known that they were doing anything wrong? Back in the days of Noah, every thought a person had was wicked. There needed to be stability in the earth. People needed to know what was acceptable in God's sight and what was not. Therefore, the Moses covenant itself with all its laws could not save people.

Another covenant was between God and King David and his descendants to be established as heirs to the throne of the nations of Israel. "And when thy days be fulfilled, and thou shalt sleep with thy fathers, I will set up thy seed after thee, which shall proceed out of thy bowels, and I will establish his kingdom. He shall build a house for my name, and I will establish the throne of his kingdom forever" (2 Samuel 7:12–13). This covenant reached its fulfillment when Jesus, a descendant of David, was born.

The Moses covenant is also referred to as the Old Testament covenant and was replaced by the New Testament covenant. The New Testament covenant made with Christ makes the difference between the covenant of the law made with Moses and the covenant of promise very clear. Under the new covenant, you are under grace.

Grace is undeserved favor. You don't work for the promises of God. Grace is known for producing change in your life. It changes you and makes you want to do what's right. If you have a desire to do right, you won't want to sin. A lot of people are misled about being righteous. Some people think that being righteous only comes about when they do things that are right when the truth is the opposite of that. You were made righteous when you gave your life to over Christ. "For he hath made him to be sin for us, who knew no sin: that we might be made righteousness of God in him" (2 Corinthians 5:21).

Because you are already righteous, you will only produce a righteous life. I said produce and not work at being righteous. Notice I did not say that you would never be tempted or have opportunities to sin. Grace does not empower you to sin. Under the new covenant, God puts His law in the inward part and writes it on a person's heart. "But this shall be the covenant that I will make with the house of Israel: After those days, saith the Lord, I will put my law in their inward parts and write it in their hearts: and will be their God, and they shall be my people" (Jeremiah 31:33).

There is still law under the new covenant of grace; it is the law of love. "A new commandment I give unto to you, That ye love one another: as I have loved you that ye also love one another. By this shall all men know that ye are my disciples, if ye love one another" (John 13:34–35).

How does God put His law in the inward part and write it on a person's heart? The law is love; when a person starts living a life of love, that person has the law of love in his or her heart. Demonstrating love can no doubt be difficult sometimes; we must not lose sight of its potential impact for witnessing in our lives. When God began working with His New Testament Christians, God gave His Holy Spirit to Israel and Gentiles alike.

God's Spirit becomes a part of your life by dwelling in you. You now have the assurance of the Holy Spirit to guide and lead as well as teach you about what to do. Receiving God's Spirit is much greater than the new covenant when Jesus ate the last supper with His disciples. He spoke of the cup and said, "This is my blood of the New Covenant which is shed for the remission of sins."

And as they were eating, Jesus took bread, and blessed it, and brake it and gave it to the disciples, and said Take eat this is my body. And took the cup and gave thanks, and gave it to them saying Drink ye all of it; For this my blood of the new testament, which is shed for many for the remission of sins. (Matthew 26:26–28)

God's Word contains literally thousands of promises that are waiting to be claimed by you in faith, obedience, and patience. All the promises that are found in the Bible belong to those who believe in His Word. The promises can only be claimed by believers. The only promise for an unbeliever is the promise of salvation. There are no broken promises. You may say, "Unfortunately, they are not working for me in my life." Though there are different promises for certain times in the Bible, you have to realize that if the promises of God are not being brought forth in your life, it has nothing at all to do with them being broken by God. He never takes back or changes His promises or Word.

God can't break covenant. "Know therefore that the Lord thy God, he is God, the faithful God, which keepeth covenant and mercy with them that love him and keep his commandments to a thousand generations" (Deuteronomy 7:9). God's promises never fail. He is faithful and a just God, and He remains faithful in everything that He has said or done.

God can't change. He is known for changing people and circumstances. "For I am the Lord, I change not: therefore ye sons of Jacob are not consumed" (Malachi 3:6). God is not a man and cannot lie. "God is not a man that He should lie: neither the son of man that he should repent: hath he said, and shall he not do it? Or hath he spoken and shall He not make it good?" (Numbers 23:19) "But as God is true our word toward you was yea and nay" (2 Corinthians 1:18).

God is faithful, trustworthy, and very dependable. You can rely on His Word no matter the circumstances, situations, or atmosphere you find yourself in. You are not living by what you see, feel, or hear if you live by the Word of God; you live by what you believe and are promised by God today. You can't live your life by what you see but by the leading of the Holy Spirit and what you have wisdom of.

You are not always going to see what's best for you, but you will know what's right for you to do. The scriptural promises are words from God that are sent forth to give comfort and rest to those who believe and live as the Spirit of God leads them to. You are never too old or young for the promises. Jesus died and left you under the guidance of the Holy Spirit, who will lead and guide you into a promising life.

Remember, the Holy Spirit was a promise to those who believe. No promises belong to only one person but to everyone who believes in God. "In whom ye also trusted, after that ye heard the Word of truth, the gospel of your salvation: In whom also after that ye believed, ye were sealed with that Holy Spirit of Promise" (Ephesians 1:3).

We are living under the new covenant. So when someone refers to you as a new covenant Christian, you should have a complete understanding of why you are one. Jesus Himself is the mediator of this better covenant between God and humanity. "And for this cause he is the mediator of the new testament, that by means of death, for the redemption of the transgressions that were under the first testament, they which are called might receive the promise of eternal inheritance" (Hebrews 9:15).

Jesus' death and His blood that was shed on the cross served as the pledge that God made to us to seal this new covenant. An unconditional agreement is between two people, but only one of the two has to do something. Nothing is required of the other person—that is being under grace. The New Testament Christians live under grace and not the law. "For sin shall not have dominion over you: for ye are not under the law but grace" (Romans 6:14).

Grace was the covenant that came into this world by Jesus Christ. "But now we are delivered from the law, that being dead wherein we were held: that we should serve in the newness of Spirit, and not in the oldness of the letter" (Romans 7:6). In the Old Testament, people were required to perform. In the New Testament, people were required to only believe and have faith.

You are a New Testament Christian who does not live your life by the laws anymore but only by the leading of Holy Spirit. In the new covenant, God promises to forgive sin. There will be a worldwide knowledge of the Lord. Jesus came to fulfill the law of Moses. "Think not that I am come to destroy the law, or the prophets: I am not come to, but to fulfil" (Matthew 5:17).

This was why the Holy Spirit was left to dwell inside you. In the New Testament covenant, the Holy Spirit never leaves you. "Howbeit when he, the Spirit of truth is come, he will guide you into all truth: for he shall not speak of himself: but whatsoever he shall hear that shall he speak: and he will shew you things to come" (John 16:13).

In the old covenant, the Holy Spirit came upon the people but He never stayed. The unconditional covenant is one in which God dedicates Himself to do what He promised to do regardless of what believers of the promise might do. You are not righteous by your good works or deeds but because God said that you are.

It's not going to come about by the flesh. The law was given to show people their sins and that they needed a Savior. It was obvious that people could not save themselves. They could not even keep the laws that were given to them. The Bible teaches that salvation has always been about faith alone, not by your works or deeds. "For by grace ye are saved through faith: and that not of yourselves: it is the gift of God. Not of works, lest any man should boast" (Ephesians 2:8–9).

The promise of salvation by faith that God made to Abraham was a part of the Abraham covenant, and it still remains in effect today. The inheritance of the promises cannot be received as payment for keeping the law. The promises of God are not private because what God has done and will do is not a secret. No promises belong to only one person but to everyone who has given his or her life over to Jesus Christ and believes what He has done. The promises belong to God's children and were given as an inheritance.

In the natural, when you are left an inheritance, you receive, acquire, or take over from another. There was nothing done on your own effort to deserve it. These promises were given to you because of who you are and what family you are a part of. You are a family member in the kingdom of God. The promises were given to you to be used now because they already belong to you. They are to be used under all and any circumstances in your life today. That is why they were given to you now on earth. You won't need them when you arrive in heaven.

Everything that God has given to you has to play a part in your life today. Faith is not going to be necessary in heaven because anyone who is going to heaven has to have faith to arrive there. "For by grace are ye saved through faith: and that not of yourselves: it is the gift of God. Not of works, lest any man should boast" (Ephesians 2:8).

Forgiveness is not required in heaven because it's a place of love. It's not a place where haters dwell. "Blessed are the peacemakers: for they shall be called the children of God." (Matthew 5:9) Healing is not demanded in your body in heaven because when you arrive, you will be given a new body. "For we know that if our earthly house of this tabernacle were dissolved, we have a building of God, a house not made with hand, eternal in the heavens" (2 Corinthians 5:1).

Deliverance is another promise not needed in your life in heaven because there is nothing there that will have you in bondage. "And the Lord shall deliver me from every evil, and will preserve me unto his heavenly kingdom: to who be glory for ever and ever Amen" (2 Timothy 4:18).

Prosperity is not required in heaven because the streets are made of gold, and there will be mansions. "And the twelve gates were twelve pearls: every several gates was of one pearl: and the streets of the city was gold, as it were transparent glass" (Revelation 21:21). "In my Father's house are many mansions: if it were not so, I would have told you I go to prepare a place for you" (John 14:2).

Love is not an option in heaven. "A new commandment I give unto you, That ye love on another as I have loved you, that ye also love one to another. By this shall all men know that ye are my disciples, I love on to another" (John 13:34–35).

These promises were given to you now because where you are now is where they are needed. We are to live our lives like we are already have the promises of God. You will go to a place in heaven where the promises of God will already be. "Thy kingdom come. Thy will be done in earth, as it is in heaven" (Matthew 6:10). They were given to the believers of the kingdom of God.

You have to be a part of the kingdom in order to obtain the promises from the King. You have to be a part of the family in order to obtain your portion of the inheritance. With the promises, we will bring others into the kingdom of God with us. We have promises for salvation of our families and households. "And they said believe on the Lord Jesus Christ, and thou shalt be saved, and thy house" (Acts 16:31).

God is willing and able to do what may seem impossible to us. And God will enable you take back what the Devil has taken away from you. How can you claim the promises of God? The promises of God are claimed by faith and patience. "That ye be not slothful, but followers of them who through faith and patience inherit the promises" (Hebrews 6:12).

If you claim the Lord's promises with a right spirit and pure motive with the correct behavior, He will honor them. You can't earn or deserve God's promises; they are yours by inheritance. They belong to you and are free because of who you are. "And if ye be Christ then ye are Abraham seed and heirs according to the promise" (Galatians 3:29).

The price that was paid in order to receive them was not cheap, and it was not paid for by you. It has already been paid for by the blood of Jesus Christ. Claiming the promises of God has nothing at all to do with your abilities or disabilities.

> And being not weak in faith, he considered not his own body now dead, when he was about an hundred years old, neither yet deadness of Sara's womb: He staggered not at the promise of God through unbelief: but was strong in faith, giving glory to God: And being fully persuaded that, what he promised, He was able to perform. (Romans 4:19–21)

Abraham had two sons; one was born by God's promise (Isaac). His birth happened because God had promised it. And another son (Ishmael) was born because of self-effort. God had told Abraham to wait, but he put off the will of God for a long time.

The promises that are given to you don't depend on your physical abilities or age. You may have situations or circumstances in life that you feel limit the promises of God. The promises are brought into your life by faith, obedience, and patience as you live under the covenant of grace. "Therefore it is of faith, that if might be by grace: to the end the promise might be sure to all the seed: not to that only which is of the law, but to that also which is of faith of Abraham: who is the father of us all" (Romans 4:16).

Abraham was one hundred years old, and Sarah was ninety years old when Isaac was born. All that was needed of Abraham and Sarah was their faith and patience for the promise of their son. Abraham had two sons by two different women; these situations actually brought him two different results. One was by self-effort and the other one by the promise of God. "For all the promises of God in him are yea, and in Him Amen, unto the glory of God by us. All the promises are yes in Christ" (2 Corinthians 1:20). "That ye be not slothful, but followers of them who through faith and patience inherit the promises" (Hebrews 6:12). Those who imitate God by faith and patience inherit the promises of God that already belong to them if they are believers in Jesus Christ.

The Promises of God

- The Promise of Salvation (Isaiah 12:2, Romans 10:9)
- The Promise of Eternal Life (John 5:24, John 6:47)
- The Promise of Faithfulness (Deuteronomy 7:8–9, Psalm 36:5)
- The Promise of Success (Proverbs 15:6, Isaiah 30:23)
- The Promises of Guidance (Psalm 32:8, Isaiah 42:16)
- The Promise of Wisdom (James 1:5, Ecclesiastes 2:26)
- The Promise of Repentance (Isaiah 30:15, Acts 3:19)
- The Promise of Mercy (Romans 12:20–21, Luke 6:36)
- The Promise of Peace (Psalm 4:8, Isaiah 26:3)
- The Promise of Prayer (Matthew 7:7–8, Matthew 21:22)
- The Promise of Protection (2 Thessalonians 3:3, Psalm 121:7–8)
- The Promise of the Holy Spirit (Proverbs 1:23, John 14:16–17)
- The Promise of Godly Citizenship (Psalm 33:12, Proverbs 21:1)
- The Promise of Money (Psalm 1:3, Isaiah 53:10)
- The Promise of Healing (Isaiah 53:5, Psalm 103:3)

Those are only a few of the thousands of promises that are located in the Bible.

There makes a tremendous difference who makes the promises to you. When God makes promises, they are never broken. The Devil approaches you with the exaggerated emphasis on the pleasure you can enjoy if you sin. He asks you to invest your time, life, and skills along with gifts and talents to things with promise of immediate return but without telling you about the risk you will be taking or other people's lives that you will destroy. The Devil will never tell you about your future when he does not need you anymore.

The Lord is not slack concerning His promises or His Word, as some people are. We are all accustomed to seeing promises be made and then broken. There may be many reasons why it happens. Sometimes we forget; sometimes we are negligent. Often, a promise is broken due to circumstances beyond our control. It's nothing but a privilege that you serve a God who keeps His Word.

The whole Bible, from the beginning to the end, has promises in it. There are two types of promises that God makes—conditional and unconditional. With unconditional promises, nothing—no situations, conditions, or weapons formed against you—can change them. They will eventually come to pass. Conditional promises are promises that He makes that solely depend on your response to them. Your response should be obedience to His Word.

God says to us, "When you move, I move; when you act, I act." Your self-effort does not make things happen. Knowing about the promises of God and knowing the will of God for your life has an effect on the outcome of the promises. In order for you to know what God's will is for your life, you must first be in the Word of God and apply it in every area of your life. God's promises do you no good if you don't believe in them.

Hebrews 4:1–2 says, "Let us therefore fear, lest a promise being left us of entering into his rest, any of you should seem to come short of it. For unto us was the gospel preached, as well as unto them: but the word preached did not profit them, not being mixed with faith in them that heard it." The children of Israel were given a promise, but they did not believe what they heard.

God's promises will not have an effective outcome unless you have the faith along with patience for the promises. It's not what happens to you in life that causes you to be defeated. It's about what you believe about your atmosphere and circumstances that makes you an overcomer.

How can you find yourself believing in the beginning and not the end of the Bible? Faith is believing in what God said that He would do and what He has already done for you. Do not believe in what you see, feel, or hear if it is not the Word of God. Believing in what God said has everything to do with you. His Word works whether you believe it or not. God said to take care of the possible and leave the impossible to Him.

What are your favorite promises? There are many different promises in the Word of God. He promises to heal you, protect you, provide for you, deliver you, and prosper you. God has anything that you could possibly imagine for you and your family and friends.

What does a promise means to you? Remember to keep your word to whoever you make a promise. Can that person rest assured that you are going to do what you said you would do? Do you think that you should promise someone something if you know deep down inside your soul that you don't have any intention to fulfill that promise? I have heard an old saying: "Promises are made to be broken." That is not in the Word of God.

There are different types of promises that people make every single day. These promises are made to each other. Every day of our lives, we are to be committed to keeping those promises. These promises were made to each other in the presence of God with others witnessing. Those promises were made for better or worse, in sickness and in health, and until death do us part. I promise to tell the truth and nothing but the truth, so help me God.

If you have already made these promises, did you really mean them? Did you stop to think, *Okay, Lord, can I really keep those promises? Am I at a point in my life where I take these promises seriously? Do I really mean what I am saying?* Before you make a promise, you should have a clear definition of what making a promise is about. What type of promises do you make—conditional or unconditional?

Making a promise to someone and not keeping them has not worked out in my favor. People depended on me to do what I told them I would do. There have been times when I failed to keep them. But when you really have the wisdom to understand the principles of keeping promises, your word becomes more dependable. It will not be difficult anymore to keep them. We have all experienced this before. But like I always remind others, you can't change what you don't confront.

If you're having trouble keeping promises, it's best for you to not make something that you know you can't bring about. Promises are very important regardless of who you make them to. God does not value one person over another; He sees everyone with love. He hates sin but loves sinners. Everybody may not be where he or she wants to be in his or her walk with Jesus Christ. But everybody in God's sight is loved and has value to Him regardless of whether he or she is an unbeliever or a saint.

The next time that you make a promise to do something for someone, don't forget that person has value in God's sight. There are just certain things that He is unable to do for and through you if are not His child. But He loves everybody unconditionally.

I learned about promises the hard way. Sometimes after doing all you can do in the flesh, all you have left in your life are the promises of God. It really should not take life situations to teach us about the promises of God, but unfortunately for some of us, that is the only way we learn about them. God promised that He will do what He said He would do.

God is very dependable; He has the power to keep His promises to His people. And He has given His people the power to receive these promises. He promised you that He would never leave you or forsake you, and He has not. "Teaching them to observe all things whatsoever I have commanded you: and lo I am with you alway, even unto the end of the world Amen" (Matthew 28:20). "Let your conversation be without covetousness: and be content with such things as ye have: for he hath said, I will never leave thee, nor forsake thee" (Hebrews 13:5).

There were times in my life when I tried everything along with everybody else; then it was time to try Jesus Christ. Sometimes it is the best thing for you to only have Jesus left in your life. If you did not, you would never really come to realize that He should be a priority in your life. You must come into the knowledge in your Spirit that He is all you have left to depend on. He is the source of all other resources in your life. All I had was His love and promises to move me forward in this journey called "life"

Don't get me wrong; we need other people in our lives. But I still have not found a human being who can do what my God has promised to do for me and to me as well as through me. Our God is someone that people are not. Our God is not a liar in any way, shape, or form—not because He wants to lie but because He cannot lie.

I am very proud to be a Girl Scout Troop Leader. I love what the Girl Scouts stand for and also how and what they are being taught. It's delightful to know that no one has to pay me to do what God has already anointed me to do. What I was born to do is much more important than what I can get paid to do. Doing what I do and only comes from the grace of God; it enables me to do what He has called me to do. I love being a part of mentoring young girls to be successful women who understand the concept of keeping a promise.

When I was approached to be a Troop Leader, I was very excited to know that I had a chance to share with others who would listen and learn. My troop has a meeting once a week, and the girls are very excited to see me as well as each other. We start our meetings with prayer. Then we move on to the Girl Scout Law, and then we quote our Girl Scout Promise. The law and the promise are verbal assurances of their word— lifelong commitments that the girls will take with them throughout their entire lives.

Teaching young girls that their words have meaning and having them put it to use in their communities shows them that they are becoming women of their word. The promise that they speak has a mission and vision of who they are becoming, regardless of other people's opinions of them.

Girl Scouts builds girls' courage, confidence, and character. The proof is in the world today. Eighty percent of women business owners were Girl Scouts. Sixty-nine percent of female US senators were Girl Scouts. Sixty-seven percent of female members of the House of Representatives were Girl Scouts.

It all started with young girls who were committed to keeping their word and Troop Leaders who were interested in promoting the Girl Scout law and promise. Troop Leaders prepare young girls to become our leaders for tomorrow by creating an atmosphere for the Girl Scout promise. The promise is not about saying one thing and doing another; it's about doing what you promised that you would do.

Being a Christian is not about saying one thing and doing another. It's about doing what was asked of you. And the Troop Leaders are committed to showing the girls how keeping your word makes a huge difference in the future for yourself as well as others.

The Bible is a book full of promises; they are conditional and unconditional. It's very important to know about the promises of God for His people because they are inherited. They already belong to you; it is not necessary to work for them. "That ye be not slothful, but followers of them who through faith and patience inherit the promises" (Hebrews 6:12).

The provisions are in the promises of God. You must live on the foundation of the promises until you see the unseen. There will come a time in your life when you are resting in the promises of God—not on the promise of a paycheck, a doctor's report, the economy, or what the government has promised to do for you. There is only one way right way for a child of God to live in this present world. That way is only by faith and obedience to the Word of God.

Sometimes difficult situations or circumstances happen to you. Danger comes our way, seen or unseen. There is one promise that God did not make to us. He did not promise us that we would not have pain on this journey. Whether you see it coming or not doesn't change what already belongs to you. It does not change what Jesus has already provided for those who believe in Him. But knowing about the promises will make a huge difference once you respond to your situations and circumstances with the Word of God.

Light conquers darkness, and a promise conquers problems. Believers live supernatural lives. You are not confined to the normal. Ephesians 6:12 teaches, "For we wrestle not against flesh and blood, but against principalities, against powers against the rulers of darkness of this world, against spiritual wickedness in high places." You are in this world but not of this world. The battle belongs to the Lord, and it is time for you to stop trying to fight the battle yourself.

People should believe and know that there is something different about you. Sometimes we accept something different but do nothing different; yet we want something different to happen to us. You have to live your entire life by faith and on the promises of God. You come against your circumstances and situations and pass your test and trails only in the spirit realm.

You can't pick and choose when it's convenient for you to live on the promises of God. Living by the promises of God is an everyday lifestyle. Everything in the kingdom of God only comes by faith. Faith comes by hearing the Word of God. "So then faith cometh by hearing, and hearing by the Word of God" (Romans 10:17).

Now it is up to you to live according to the Word of God. When you place your faith in God's promises for your life, you will have a desire in your heart for the promises of God to be brought forth in other people's lives as well. There comes revealed knowledge that the way you are currently living is not how you were promised to live if you are not living by the Word of God.

You should only want the best for others also. When that desire is deep in your soul, you can't help but start to create an atmosphere for the promises of God. When you are in Christ, you are not selfish. Others should be a concern to you, and when you begin to see the supernatural transfer into the natural, your objective should be to help others obtain the promises that belong to them.

Do not overlook the responsibility that you have as a Christian to bring forth the Word of God into your atmosphere. You can't have a testimony of something that you have not experienced. I can't testify to anyone about the promises of God in my life if I have not experienced them.

God spoke to my spirit to do something, but the money was not lining up with what I was told to do. I live my life by faith. I did not even consider how the funds were going to come about. I was too busy focusing on being obedient to what I was told to do. Isaiah 26:3 says, "Thou wilt keep him in perfect peace, whose mind is stayed on thee: because he trusteth in thee." I had peace with what God spoke to me about, and others did not.

There will be carnal-minded people in your atmosphere. They will try to talk you out of what the Lord has told you to do because it does not line up with what they see at the time. I was told, "Well, you should wait until you have the funds; then pursue what the Lord has told you to do."

The Lord spoke to my spirit and said, "If you wait until you receive the funds, that is not faith. I promised you that I will provide for you, and have I not been a provider?" Of course, I was obedient to the Lord regardless of how things looked and what others said was best for me to do.

Knowing what's best and what's right for you to do are two totally different things. That means that you will receive two different results. If God tells me to do something, then He has the power to bring it to pass. So going forth in doing what I was told also helped me to create an atmosphere for the promises of God for those who were around me. They saw that God did what He said He would do. There was no doubt in my mind that it would not work out in my favor. "And we know that all things work together for the good to them that love God, to them who are the called according to His purpose" (Romans 8:28).

After what I was told to do came to pass and I did not lack anything financially, I had an opportunity to show those within my atmosphere that when I have a need, He has the supply. Philippians 4:19 says, "But my God shall supply all your needs according to his riches in glory by Christ Jesus." This situation opened up doors for others who were in my atmosphere to see the supernatural manifested in the natural. But I had to know that God would do what He said He would do.

God is not lacking concerning His promises to us. All you have to do is put the promises to work in your life. The factor that determines whether I receive them or not is me. I know that sometimes you can fear things not working out the way you planned them to. But you must be sure that you include God in the plans. Sometimes you make plans in your life and want Him to bless them but take no time to seek Him first.

If God has given you a vision of something to do, there will always be a spirit of fear of things not working out or a reason why you should not do it. Second Timothy 1:6–7 teaches, "Wherefore I put thee in remembrance that thou stir up the gift of God, which is in thee by the putting on of my hands. For God hath not given us the spirit of fear: but of power and of love and of a sound mind."

The enemy will always try to use fear in your life. You should not let fear be a factor in your life because of who you are. Knowing who you are plays a huge role in your life today. Ask yourself, *What does God think about me?*

What happened to you has nothing to do with who you are. There are times in our lives when we confuse who we are with what we been through. Your circumstances have nothing to do with who you are. You are the righteousness of God when you become born again. You receive God's gracious free gift of righteousness, which is right standing with Him. The only thing you ever have to do to receive this free gift is to accept it. You receive it by faith, just as you receive the free gift of salvation. God only wants you to develop your faith until you trust Him more than you trust yourself and others.

Another promise that should always keep your mind-set in focus is in Romans 8:28: "And we know that all things works together for good to them that love, God to them who are called according to his purpose." When you are a true child of God, you will always find the treasure in the plan that did not work in your favor. God's promises are to be obtained by His children in this life. You can't say something does not work for you if have not tried it.

You will never know how something works if you don't believe it. You will just be in a position to assume how it is supposed to work. People don't believe the will of God for their lives because they try to understand it in order to believe it. I learned that you have to believe it to understand it. That's why you have to know about the promises for yourself. It is all right to hear about them from others who have used them. It makes a huge difference when you know they work for you.

In my situation, I knew that they worked, and I was not trying to hear anything that was in opposition to what the Lord told me to do. When you know that they work like that, you will become the same exact way. All it takes is just one promise to be brought about in your life, and the rest will be history.

God promised to love you, protect you, and bring you into the knowledge and wisdom of His Word. Start to focus on what already belongs to you and not what happened to you. It will make life less stressful than trying to make it happen in your own effort. You just can't do what God can. We waste over half of our lives trying to bring forth what only God can do.

Make an effort to live your life only by the promises. You do not have to work to have them. They are not things that you deserved, and nobody can hinder from you having them. Remember that the promised life was given to you by someone who can always keep promises—someone who has the power to keep them.

Book Notes

1. What is the definition of a promise?

2. What types of covenants are there?

3. Which covenant are you under?

4. What are the conditions for having the promises of God manifested in your life?

5. Who can claim the promises of God?

6. What are some of the promises that you currently claim?

CHAPTER 6

Maintaining the Atmosphere

Now that you have established the revealed knowledge of creation, atmosphere, climate, and promises in your life and after you have started to create a Godly atmosphere, you will have to learn how to maintain the atmosphere and climate that allow God's promises to be brought forth. It takes power to subsist in this life.

Having power is not about how much you have or don't have. The power is within you regardless of what you have. You brought nothing into this world, and you are not going to take anything out of it. "For we brought nothing into this world and it is all certain we can carry nothing out" (1 Timothy 6:7). If there are requirements for obtaining the promises, there must be requirements for keeping them.

The *New World Dictionary* defines the word maintain as "to keep or keep up: carry on to keep in continuance or in a certain state." Once you have started to maintain that Godly atmosphere in your life, it is going to be a vital part of your journey. You cannot commit to maintaining a Godly atmosphere only when you feel like it. It's not done when it's convenient for you or dependent on how others treat you. It's not to be put into practice one day of the week when you go to church and left out the rest of the week.

What you do after church determines whether the kingdom of God works. You do not receive salvation because you are part of the church, sing in the church choir, in prison ministry, or volunteer to feed the homeless or drive the church van. You do not maintain the atmosphere for the promises of God just because you go the church and Sunday school on Sundays and Bible studies on Wednesdays. You have a relationship and not a religion.

Honoring a relationship with Christ the Messiah has to be a mind-set. You must fix your mind on the things of the kingdom in order to receive a kingdom response.

> Finally brethren whatsoever things are true, whatsoever things are honest, whatsoever things are just, whatsoever things are pure, whatsoever things are lovely, whatsoever things are of good report: if there be any virtue, and if there be any praise, think on these things. Those things, which ye have both learned, and received, and heard and seen in me do: and the God of peace shall be with you. (Philippians 4:8–9)

Before you have a changed life, you must have a changed mind. "And be not conformed to this world: but be ye transformed by the renewing of the mind, that ye may prove what is good and acceptable, and perfect will of God" (Romans 12:2). When you think like Christ, then you can live like Him. It's a daily commitment and a lifestyle that is created and maintained every single day.

Maintaing is how your life is lived outside the church. When nobody is looking, are you still doing right things? When nobody is listening, are you saying only what the Word of God said? You should follow God all the time, regardless of how you feel, your atmosphere, circumstances, situations, physical disabilities, or age. How can you expect to receive the promises of your heavenly Father when you have not prepared yourself for them? If you are not prepared to receive what the Lord has for you, then you will not be in a position to keep it.

You don't have to get ready for an opportunity when you see one coming. Maintaining the Word is about already being in the position for the doors of opportunity when they open up to you. If the atmosphere has already been created and maintained by you, then all that's left to do is receive what rightly belongs to you anyway. The plan is for you to be ready way before the opportunity comes to you. "And Joshua said unto the people, Sanctify yourselves: for to morrow the Lord will do wonders among you" (Joshua 3:5).

Healing, prosperity, deliverance, blessing, and God's protection already belong to you. There are a lot of principals that should be applied in your life. You have to first give your life over to Jesus Christ, and He will be your Lord and Savior. You must be filled with the Holy Spirit. You are required to make Jesus a priority in your life. The life of a Christian is led by the Holy Spirit.

You must learn that you cannot just fit Jesus Christ into your schedule. You must schedule your time around Him and allow His will for your life come about. You cannot let anything or anyone convince you that Jesus should not be first in your life. Jesus Christ should actually be first in everything that you do and say. He should also be first in every area of your life.

I had to learn to trust Jesus in everything that I did, not just in the areas that were convenient for me. There were times when it appeared to me that doing certain things would not really benefit me. Of course, at that time, I was looking at life in the natural. Living by faith will mean living in the supernatural; living by the world's system will mean living by your five senses. The promises of God are not going to come about by the flesh but by His supernatural power. But I don't live my life by what I see anymore.

When you learn to trust in the Lord, you will then begin to move beyond your understanding. "Trust ye in the Lord forever: for in the Lord JEHOVAH is everlasting strength" (Isaiah 26:4). Sometimes you might just have to shut your mind off and simply believe. When you have reached a place in your life where you believe everything belongs to God, you will stop trying to figure everything else out. When I stepped out in faith and let God work for me, God did not fail me.

I had to learn how to maintain in my life what the Word taught me. Just as God is committed to doing what He said He would do, I had to commit to do what He asked and given me instructions to do. One of His instructions for His people is to always seek Him first. "But seek ye first the kingdom of God, and his righteousness: and all these things shall be added" (Matthew 6:33).

In all things, you have to experience God to know that He is not a liar. The word of God teaches that you already have power pertaining to life.

> According as his divine power hath given unto us all things that pertain unto life and godliness, through the knowledge of him that called us to glory and virtue: Whereby are given unto us exceeding great and precious promises: that by these you might be partakes of the divine nature, having escaped the corruption that is in the world through lust. (2 Peter 1:3–4)

So if you already have what it takes, then what's taking you so long to put it into action? In order for you to believe the promises of God that already belongs to you, you first have to believe in who He says He is. If you don't believe in God, how are going to believe in what He says about you? Then you won't believe in what He said He will do for you.

It's not hard for us to believe in what others say about different people. Why is it so hard to believe what our God has said about us? If you don't believe what He has said about you, then you definitely are not going to believe what He has already done for you on the cross. He did not say, "Understand how and when the promises will come." He said to just simply believe and have faith along with patience in the unseen. "That ye be not slothful, but followers of them who through faith and patience inherit the promises" (Hebrews 6:12).

Creating an atmosphere for the unseen takes faith, time, patience, and diligence. Proverbs teaches you that diligence is something that has to be obtained in your soul. "The soul of the sluggard desirth, and hath nothing: but the soul of the diligent shall be made fat" (Proverbs 13:4).

Maintaining your atmosphere is not going to always be easy. It's going to be a fight and not a walk in the park. Satan's forces are not invincible; they can sometimes seem so because of our ignorance toward the Word of God. Maintaining the Word will not allow the spirits of rebellion, disobedience, selfishness, or reasoning to control us or the atmospheres that we are in. But the good news is that you are already on the winning side.

You have the option to be a powerful Christian or a pitiful one, but you can't be both. What you have to do is turn God's promises into a daily confession. Refuse to live your life any other way than powerfully when you receive the wisdom of the power that you already have, and believe it already belongs to you. Then there will be no situations, circumstances, issues, or problems that are going to limit your spirit or the promises of God from being manifested in your life. There can be limits on your physical body but never your spirit. The inner person has no limit.

Patience is another necessity for maintaining the atmosphere. Having patience will consist of believing Scripture and applying it to your everyday life. Being a Christian requires you to renew your mind, to renew your mind is exchanging your thoughts for God's thoughts. That is a continual process that is necessary until the Lord calls you home.

You must set your mind according to the Word of God in order to carry it out. You have to become a maker and maintainer of the Word of God. If you continue to think the way you always thought, you will have what you always had. When you make God's way of doing things your way, then you reap the manifestation of the kingdom of God. The Word is Spirit, and walking in the Spirit is a mind-set that is aligned with the Word of God.

Maintaining the atmosphere that God has already created for you is going to require the same continual process. Life is a process, and the Word of God only takes you and others who come in contact with Him to the next level. In the kingdom of God, it's about moving forward and not backward. It's not about you anymore; it's about God and others. Creating this Godly atmosphere draws others into the kingdom of God—especially those who you have tried to share the Word of God with, even if they have refused to listen to you.

When you share the good news of the gospel with others, there is only one motive that will be achieved. You are sharing wisdom with others not out of duty but of love. If someone did not love you, he or she would not bother to tell you something that would change your life for the better. If Jesus did not love us, He would have not given His life for us or told us about a better way of life. He died for you, and you live for Him.

Of course, you run into people or who just do not listen to anything you have to say about the Word of God. That's another critical point where maintaining a Godly atmosphere for the promises of God works out not only in your favor, but also for others who reject the good news of the gospel. God does not bless division; where unity is, there will be anointing and blessings. One of Satan's foremost tactics is to divide and conquer. There has to be someone in your household to create an atmosphere for the promises of God. The ability to maintain what is required of them brings about unity in the home.

We have to remind ourselves from time to time that the Devil will use anybody to try to keep our focus off of God and doing work for His kingdom. The Devil wants to disturb any place where anyone has peace. He does not want you or anyone in your atmosphere to obtain anything that already belongs to you and your family. All he supports is disuniting—dividing or separating.

The Devil's agenda is to always bring about disorganization. That is why you must have the mind of Christ and a mind-set only for the kingdom of God. You can show some people better than you can tell them. I am a living witness that maintaining a Godly atmosphere has not only changed me, but also those I love and those I come in contact with on a daily basis.

God is the source of unlimited blessing and promises that should flow from your life into the lives of others. Creating an atmosphere for the promises of God is basically living the Word of God out to its fullest. The Bible teaches that you are the salt of the earth and the light of the world. "Let your light so shine before men, that they may see your good works and glorify your Father which is in heaven" (Matthew 5:16).

The word of God has to be taught and also experienced. Only one experience of what God will do completely changes you for the rest of your life. From that point on, you will become a totally different person. You will find yourself wanting to experience all the things your heavenly Father has for your life. You will also want others to have the same experience that you have with Jesus. You will look at life in another direction, and from that point on, all you want to do is tell others of the wonderful, awesome, on-time God that you serve.

Sometimes you are going to run into people who think that you are a little weird because you are in love with God and His Word. But if being in love with Jesus is considered being weird, then I am guilty. You must learn that if you don't stand for something, you will fall for anything. But if you don't continue to maintain that Godly atmosphere and set the correct conditions for your climate, it will only make your walk with the Lord a struggle. It can make your journey a little difficult and hinder the promises that already belong to you.

God does not want you to live your life like hell and then go to heaven. How are you going to be comfortable in a heavenly atmosphere if all you knew about was struggling, lack, frustration, depression, and defeat? I had to learn that the more time I stayed focused on what was wrong in my life, the more I produced wrong things. Once you come to a place in life where you have true knowledge that you no longer have to make things happen—that they are brought about—you really don't need your plans. God already has a plan for your life and His plan is always much better for you.

Maintaining an atmosphere could be better expressed as being a doer of the Word and not just a hearer. That's the only way to have the victory that God has already provided for you. God has an unchanging oath with His people. You can't be lazy when it comes to maintaining the Word of God. Being a disciple has many requirements—having love, faith, and patience. "A new commandment I give unto you, That ye love one another: as I have loved you, that ye also love one another. By this shall all men know that ye are my disciples, if ye have love one to another" (Matthew 13:34–35).

Many people want to pray and beg God to help them. But they don't want to do things His way. When His Word says to do something, it has to be done regardless of how you feel about it, what it looks like, or what others may think about you when you do it. When you allow God to work, the Word of God will change your life as well as the lives of others.

People are going to want what you have. But not everybody will be willing to do what you did to receive it. The promises will also change your circumstances. Change can be defined as "to become or make different." Changes come about in two different ways; they are brought about, or you can make them happen. If you were not interested in change, you would not have picked up this book. Change brings about a better person in you, better decisions, and a totally different way of living. Change brings about a different atmosphere and climate.

You must remember that the influence you are under determines what type of changes are going to come about in your life. The climate is what you expect, and the weather is what you get. When you realize that changes can and will affect others, it not only benefits you to change for the better, but also others. All changes have to be maintained. Keeping up with what you decide to do, whether it is in the natural or supernatural, is required from you. Your part in this journey is to keep up with what Christ has already done for you.

You now have to learn how to be in the background. Take a back seat, and allow the Holy Spirit to lead you through life. It can be very difficult when you are used to doing it yourself and your way. The Lord had to show me that being in the background was necessary and not always a bad thing.

I was diagnosed with a medical condition that kept me from driving. I had been driving myself since I was a teenager. But I was not allowed to drive anymore, which means that my husband and older kids have to take me places and pick me up. I can't even begin to tell you how stressful that was. In the past, when I was ready to go somewhere, I did not have to ask anybody for permission. I did not have to worry about anyone waiting on me or me waiting for someone to come back and pick me up. In the past, if I wanted to go somewhere, I simply got in the car and went.

I had to realize that I was not in total control anymore. It took me a very long time to come to a place where I accepted that. Looking out the window at two cars in the driveway with no license to take them out of the yard was difficult and tempting. There were times when I took the car down the street to the store or somewhere that was not far from my house. Taking the car down the street would have led me to taking it across town. I believe that God was showing me what being led by the Spirit is like. You are no longer in control, but God is. Your life is led by Him. You will not always do what you feel like doing when you want to do it. It's not about doing what you want to do; it's about doing what's right because you are now under the leadership of the Holy Spirit.

When I took the car, that only showed that I lacked self-discipline and was using my self-effort. That's why you should make it a habit to think right thoughts and not reason. I began to think it wouldn't hurt to just go down the street or around the corner. You can sometimes give more control to the most unstable part of yourself, the mind, attitude and body. The Spirit controls the mind, attitude and body of a believer.

With our minds, we tend to exercise the power of reasoning along with self-effort. You will only conceive your own ideas and judgment. To have the mind of Christ, we must think like Him. God's will for my life was healing first. He promised me healing, and then I could drive again. The soul must be disciplined and mature so that the rest of your being can prosper. I did not maintain what the law of my state told me to do in the natural. Healing was one of the unconditional promises that took place on the cross. "But he was wounded for our transgression, he was bruised for our iniquities: the chastisement of our peace was upon him: and with his stripes we are healed" (Isaiah 53:5).

Patience was something that I had to work on. We all know what happens when we do what we are told not to do. It may work for a while, but it will eventually come to an end. Along with choices come consequences. Driving was not about me anymore; I had a family to think about. What would happen to my family if I said, "They are not going to tell me I can't drive"? I probably would be writing this book from somewhere I would not want to be. The Lord had to show me that I am not always going to be in control.

God wants to bring you to a place where self-effort comes to an end. That is why maintaining an atmosphere takes self-discipline and less self-effort. I was looking at it in the natural, but I was always provided transportation wherever I needed to go. The Lord had to show me this. If you take the background and let Him lead, He will provide for you. This is the very reason He sent Holy Spirit. The Holy Spirit can lead and guide you through this life.

I had the support of my family and friends for transportation, but I wanted to drive. The Lord always provided a way for me as well as for my family. In this life, you can't have it both ways. It's God's way or the highway. Your way might work for a while, but sooner or later, if something does not uplift God's kingdom, it will come to an end.

Maintaining a Godly atmosphere may not always be easy. Sometimes you start out with good intentions, but when things become difficult and challenging, it may seem easier to do it your way or just quit. This is why you need the Word of God in your life. You can't be a part of something when you have no idea how it works. You will never be able to obtain the mind of Christ by relying on your own thoughts, imagination, emotions, attitudes, or words. If you are a part of something and have no idea how it works, you can rest assured that it is not going to work out in your favor.

If you learn how to maintain the Word of God in your life, it only has one outcome, and that outcome works in your favor. Maintaining a Godly atmosphere actually makes a difference in other people's lives. Always remember that kingdom living is not only about what God can do for you, but also what you can do for God and others. Keep up, and continue in the Word of God. The more time you spend with God, the more you will produce the right type of fruit.

Growing strong and straight and having good posture works for the body. The Word of God helps your soul grow stronger and your mind think right thoughts. Proteins are nutrients that help your body to grow and repair itself. The Word of God gives nutrients to help your soul grow stronger and line up. Just like it is necessary to maintain the correct vitamins and nutrients for a stronger body, the same is required for the Word of God for your soul. "A wise man is strong: yea a man of knowledge increaseth strength" (Proverbs 24:5).

God gave you food for the body and for the soul. Both natural and supernatural things have to be maintained by you. Learning how to maintain a Godly atmosphere takes discipline, duty, and devotion. We want success in our lives but only with a minimum effort. Success comes with a price, and the price is discipline—training that develops strict self-control to enforce obedience. Next we have duty—doing what you ought to do, not what you feel like doing. Duty will not work without discipline. Last we have devotion—being loyal, faithful, and strongly devoted to something or someone. These are just a few of requirements to maintaining a Godly atmosphere.

Creating an atmosphere for the promises of God is your responsibility. Maintaining the Godly atmosphere is also a requirement. Living the life that God has promised you is your call. If you don't change the way you think, then it will create the same atmosphere in your life. You have to set your mind and keep it set in the Word of God and His promises for your life and the lives of others. You have to realize why maintaining the atmosphere is vital to life. "Through wisdom is a house builded: and by understanding it is established: And by knowledge shall the chambers be filled with all precious and pleasant riches" (Proverbs 24:3–4).

You can go deeper into the Word of God. But always remember that when you study and meditate on God's Word, you are not doing Him a favor. He already knows the Word. He knows your thoughts before you do. He already knows what you need before you need it. Your responsibility is to respond to what He has already promised you.

Always make sure that you keep your mind-set on the promises and not the problems. When people play the lottery, they have a winner's mind-set. They already know how, when, and where they are going to spend their rewards. Their minds are set on being multimillionaires. As a child of God, your mind-set should be on what already belongs to you—not on what you might get but what you already have.

You are going to believe God or the enemy. Remember, in spiritual warfare, the mind is the battlefield where the Devil makes his attacks. He knows that even though a person attends church services, if that person can't keep his or her mind on what is taught, he or she will leave out of the service the same way he or she walked in. That's why maintaining your atmosphere is a requirement in life.

Book Notes

1. What is the definition of maintaining?

2. How do you maintain your atmosphere?

3. What are the requirements of maintaining your atmosphere?

4. Does maintaining your atmosphere require a certain mind-set?

5. Do you believe that maintaining your atmosphere is a lifestyle?

CHAPTER 7

Kingdom Living

There are two kingdoms, and you live in one of them. "No man can serve two masters: for either he will hate the one, and love the other; or else he will hold to the one, and despise the other. ye cannot serve God and mammon" (Matthew 6:24). God the father has a kingdom. The King is God; He is sovereign, omnipotent, omniscient, omnipresent, and the ruler of all creation. His kingdom is called the kingdom of God. It is a realm that born-again Christians live in; it's a spiritual kingdom.

Every kingdom has a king. A king is known as one who's in authority. But you can't have authority if you don't position yourself to be under authority. The kingdom of God has angels, servants who worship and obey the commands of the King. God rules His kingdom by His own divine nature. The nature that you were born with will not enter the kingdom of God unless it is changed to His nature.

In the kingdom of God, you are not forced, tricked, or deceived into doing anything for the purpose of the kingdom. When you are in the kingdom of God, there is a certain way of doing things. How He does anything is how He does everything. Everything in the kingdom of God functions by faith.

Satan has a kingdom of darkness. The kingdom of darkness has demons who always oppose what God is doing for and through you. There are certain principles that a servant lives by in the kingdom of God. Those principles will determine how powerful your citizenship will be in the kingdom of God. There are servants who do just the minimum to make it to heaven. Others have a mission to take everybody else with them. The agenda is always going to be the same to—seek the kingdom of God first. "But seek ye first the kingdom of God, and his righteousness: and all these things shall added be unto you" (Matthew 6:33).

Go out into the world, and make disciples. There are certain benefits that the King provides for his servants. Being a part of the kingdom has its benefits. In the kingdom of darkness, you are used to try to tear down the kingdom of God. To live in the kingdom of God, you have to be a part of the kingdom and also participate in the keeping it. Kingdom living is serving God; you must have a relationship with the king you serve. You cannot just know of Him or about Him but must know Him personally by experiencing Him. We are not owners of the kingdom but stewards of God. He trusts us with His power, time, gifts, and talents. God works in partnership with His people.

You must know the kingdom that you are a part of. It's up to you to study of the rights and duties of citizenship in the kingdom of God. Kingdom living means becoming a part of a lifestyle that Jesus Christ once lived. You have to know how to become a part of the kingdom of God. What is required of your for citizenship in the kingdom of God? "And saying, Repent ye: for the kingdom of heaven is at hand" (Matthew 3:2).

You can't live in a kingdom if you are not a part of it. How can you enter the kingdom of God?

Jesus answered and said unto him, Verily, Verily, I say unto thee, Except a man be born again, he cannot see the kingdom of God. Nicodemus saith unto him, How can a man be born when he is old? Can he enter the second time into his mother's womb, and be born? Jesus answered, Verily, Verily, I say unto thee, Except a man be born of water and of the spirit, he cannot enter into the kingdom of God. (John 3:3–5)

When you enter the kingdom of God, you then become a citizen for eternity. The citizenship always remains open to those who are willing to submit their lives over to the king and are in fellowship with Him. The kingdom of God is universal; it includes angles and humans. It is eternal and spiritual and requires a relationship with the King.

The kingdom of God is in effect now—it is true. God reigns and rules over His kingdom now. "And said, Behold, I see the heavens opened, and the Son of man standing on the right hand of God" (Acts 7:56). Once you have citizenship in the kingdom of God, you must sustain a kingdom mind-set. You have to change your mentality and set it differently—not just with positive thinking. You can't have positive thinking without renewing your mind. Nothing from nothing will leave you with nothing.

When you prepare yourself in the Lord and understand the divine nature of the kingdom, you begin to learn how to hold your ground. "This I say then, Walk in the Spirit, and ye shall not fulfill the lust of the flesh" (Galatians 5:16). When you live in the kingdom of God, you are a servant of the kingdom.

There is a spiritual kingdom where God rules in the heart of every believer. This is an invisible kingdom. "And he said, Unto you it is given to know the mysteries of the kingdom of God: but to others in parables: that seeing they might not see, and hearing they might not understand" (Luke 8:10). "He answered and said unto them, because it is given unto you to know the mysteries of the Kingdom of heaven, but to them it is not given" (Matthew 13:11).

When you reject God's invitation into His kingdom, you are choosing the kingdom of darkness. If you live in the kingdom of darkness, you are a slave to the Devil. Anything he controls, he destroys. A servant is one who is employed to care for someone or his or her property. A slave is one who is completely subject to another habit or influence. If you are a slave, the Devil has you under his control. These two kingdoms have two entirely different agendas with different destinations that will bring about different lifestyles.

Your life on earth will be under the rule of God or Satan. The lifestyle in the kingdom of God will be a life of faith love, peace, joy, power, and forgiveness.

What is kingdom living? Kingdom living is a teaching ministry that was created for servants of love to teach others about the body of Christ. In the kingdom, you will live by faith in the Word and the promises of God. Kingdom living is not a church, denomination, religion, or nonprofit organization. Being in the kingdom of darkness brings about a life that is lived in envy, division, jealousy, corruption, unforgiveness, and self-effort. If you are in the kingdom of darkness, you will eventually take on the nature of the Devil.

Remember, you will always act like the people you hang out with the most. You can't have authority over the Devil when you act like him. The sooner you learn that, the better you will be. When you read, study, and meditate on the Word of God, you will learn the identity of those whose will not inherit the kingdom of God.

Know ye not that the unrighteous shall not inherit the kingdom of God? Be not deceived: neither fornicators, nor idolaters, nor adulterers, nor effeminate, nor abusers of themselves with mankind. Nor thieves, nor covetous, nor drunkards, nor revilers, nor extortioners shall inherit the kingdom of God. (1 Corinthians 6:9–10)

In order for you to inherit the kingdom of God, you first have to take the right path in life. "Enter ye in at the strait gate: for wide is the gate and broad is the way that leaded to destruction, and many there be which go in thereat: Because strait is the gate, and narrow is the way, which leadeth unto life, and few there be that find it" (Matthew 7:13–14).

A path must be chosen in life. "Thou wilt shew me the path of life: in thy presence is the fulness of joy: at thy right hand there are pleasures for evermore" (Psalm 16:11). Jesus indicated that the kingdom of God is something that you must receive in this life. "Verily I say unto you Whosoever shall not receive the kingdom of God as a little child, he shall not enter therein" (Mark 10:15).

Being in the presence of God is going to bring about the fullness of joy and pleasures into your life. "He restored my soul; he leadeth me in the paths of righteousness for His name's sake" (Psalm 23:3). Your soul is being restored, and you are being led on a certain path by the Holy Spirit. It is obvious that there is more to benefit from choosing the kingdom of God than being a slave in the kingdom of darkness. Life consists of one or the other.

Choosing the path of life or death, good or bad, right or wrong, blessed or cursed, being a servant or a slave, being wise or being a fool. You can be a powerful servant or a powerless slave. You also can be responsible for lifting the kingdom of God up or assisting in trying to tear it down. You can't have both, but you are a part of one. You either accept Jesus Christ or reject Him. The kingdom you choose is totally your decision.

God has set before you life or death; you choose the path that you will take. Once you come on the Lord's side, you will be powerful. The kingdom of God does not force itself upon anyone. I did not say that you choose what will happen to you while taking this path. But as a servant in the kingdom of God, you have assurance that whatever happens to you has already been taken care of by the blood of Jesus.

"Nay, in all things we are more than conquerors through him that loved us" (Romans 8:37). That's the kind of king you serve—one who cares about His servants and what happens to them. And if something unexpected does happen, He provides you with an answer.

Once you become a part of the kingdom of God, there is only one way servants live. That is the abundant life with power, forgiveness of sins, faith healing, blessings, prosperity, deliverance, and everything that His blood was shed for. Kingdom living is a lifestyle that testifies to others that you are a part of a kingdom that wants only the best in every area of your life.

If your life testifies to this kind of living, others will soon want to be a part of the kingdom that you are a part of. The life that you live will become a magnet. It will start to draw others to you and attract them to your presence. They will want to serve the King you serve.

You are not required to wait for your arrival in heaven to live a life that has already been promised to you on earth. The promises that we have now on earth have already been manifested in heaven. You don't have to wait for healing. In heaven, you won't need healing; you will receive a new body. You don't have to wait for prosperity; you won't need it in heaven, as the streets are made of gold. That atmosphere is already set once you find out the will for your life here.

It is plainly known that God's will for you on earth is the same will for you in heaven. "Thy kingdom come. Thy will be done in earth, as it is in heaven" (Matthew 6:10). You should not have to wait until your arrival in heaven for healing, deliverance, prosperity, blessing, and everything God has promised you now. What would be the purpose of promising you something now that you would have to wait for?

There is no need for anything in heaven but your presence. "And I will give unto thee the keys of the kingdom of heaven: and whatsoever thou shalt bind on earth shall be bound in heaven: and whatsoever thou shalt loose on earth shall be loosed in heaven" (Matthew 16:19). God could just wait until you are in heaven to give you the promises. But they already belong to you now. You don't have to wait to your arrival in heaven to live the kingdom life.

The Bible teaches us that the kingdom of God is not of this world. It does not say that you cannot have kingdom living while you are on earth. "Jesus answered, My kingdom is not of this world: if my kingdom were of this world, then would my servants fight, that I should not be delivered to the Jews: but now is my kingdom not from hence" (John 18:36).

You may ask yourself, Okay, if the kingdom of God is not here, where is it located? "And when he was demanded of the Pharisee, when the kingdom of God should come, he answered them and said, The kingdom of God cometh not with observation: Neither shall they say, Lo here: or, lo there: for behold, the kingdom of God is within you" (Luke 17:20–21). Kingdom living is a lifestyle that requires team work along with team effort. While on earth Jesus had a team that included His disciples. Together they accomplished the will of God for the kingdom. Jesus could have done it alone, but working as team everyone has a part in changing other people's lives. Team work makes the dream works for everyone.

You are the kingdom of God; it is in you. Heaven is the place of your eternal residence. If everything in the kingdom operates by faith, you are required to live a supernatural life that is lived only by the Word of God through the leading of the Holy Spirit. Christ died for healing, deliverance, prosperity, and blessings. These things already belong to you and your family.

Once you come to the Lord's side and learn your true identity, then you will know the power that you have. There is no way you can speak to the Devil if you don't have any power behind your words. You have been given the keys to the kingdom.

Kingdom living means becoming a part of a lifestyle that Jesus lived and died for you to have. Jesus came to earth, and He lived a life that only glorified His Father. He only created one type of atmosphere everywhere He went, whether He was around people who believed or people who did not believe. He had the same response for all.

Being a part of something that you only heard about but fail to believe and understand does not work in your favor. I worked in customer service before the Lord called me into ministry. Customer service requires you to work with, around, and for people. Meeting other people's needs was the priority. It had nothing to do with how they looked, how they dressed, what they had or did not have, if they were rude or nice, or if they had a nice or bad attitude. It was all about meeting the needs of the customers.

To be able to work in customer service, that's the understanding you must know about. It can't be something you heard about doing. You must understand that everybody is not going to have a nice day. But your job is not determined by how other people's days may be or how they treat or talk to you. Your job is determined by how you treat them regardless of how they treat you. If you fail to understand that, then you will fail to keep your job.

The kingdom of God and the example that Christ set for us are the same. Regardless of who you come in contact with, you will have the same response Jesus did. Do not treat anybody differently because of what they have or do not have. Our heavenly Father does not treat people differently. Living in the kingdom of God is the same. "For there is no respect of persons with God" (Romans 2:11). You can't be a part of something that you do not understand. If you do not understand it, how would you know if you were doing something in your life that your King would not approve of?

If you don't understand that you are the righteousness of God through faith in Jesus Christ, it is vital that you live your life like Jesus did. You must create an atmosphere in your life that represents the kingdom of God. When you prepare yourself with the Word of God and believe with understanding the nature of the kingdom of God, you will begin to learn to stand your ground. Christ lived a life that only glorified His Father. He created an atmosphere in His life that gave faith to those around Him. Like in customer service, your responsibility is to have the same response.

Being a part of the kingdom of God is a decision that will be life-changing not only to you, but also to anyone who comes in contact with you. When you are in the presence with unbelievers, you will sometimes be the closet to God that they may ever come. Always remember that God blesses you so that you become a blessing to someone else. Tell everyone about the King you serve. If people won't listen, then let your life be a testimony of the kingdom that you are a part of.

How can your life be a testimony of the kingdom of God? Simply create an atmosphere for the promises of God. Actions can sometimes speak much louder than words, but words have a powerful effect. Sometimes it may be better to show others than to tell them. But no doubt about it, sooner or later, they will get it.

No matter what others say or do, your citizenship can not be overridden or revoked by a simple case of mistaken identity. There will be no mistake whose kingdom you are a part of. You live by the kingdom system and not the world's. God is the source of unlimited promises and blessings that should flow from your life into the lives of others. The kingdom of God is a spiritual kingdom and not a physical organization.

Book Notes

1. How many kingdoms are there?

2. How can you obtain citizenship?

3. Where is the kingdom of God located?

4. Does your life testify what kingdom you are a part of?

5. Will you bring others into the kingdom of God with you?

Three Things to Remember and Study

1. How to renew the mind constantly
2. How to learn the way of the Spirit
3. How to walk in the Spirit

In This Book, Your Goals Should Be to:

1. Identify your atmosphere
2. Begin to create a Godly atmosphere in your life
3. Know what's required to maintain your Godly atmosphere
4. Compare your Godly atmosphere with the physical atmosphere
5. Understand how physical features can influence your Godly atmosphere
6. Focus more on promises than on problems
7. Start using your energy for faith and not for fear
8. Study your requirements and duties for citizenship in the kingdom
9. Know whether the atmosphere that you are presently in can be changed
10. Decide whose influence you will remain under
11. Set your mind to live by faith on the promises of God

PRAYER

Lord, help me to create an atmosphere that will uplift Your kingdom today. I will fix my mind on creating Your godly atmosphere and bringing about all the promises that You died for me to have. Let Your Word do a mighty work within me. Use me, Lord, as a vessel for creating an atmosphere in which my family and I will receive the promises that belong to me. Let me create an atmosphere in which others will see Christ in me.

O Lord, place me in the path of those who need to become citizens of Your kingdom. Bless me, O Lord, so that I can be a blessing to someone else. Teach me, Lord, whatever it is that I need to know about creating my atmosphere so I can make a change. Help my behavior to line up with what I speak into the atmospheres; let Your Word change me. I give You praise, glory, and honor in Jesus' name. Amen.